Madame Guyon

Also by Phyllis Thompson

TO THE HEART OF THE CITY
THE GIDEONS
AN UNQUENCHABLE FLAME
MR LEPROSY
THE RAINBOW OR THE THUNDER
CHINA: THE RELUCTANT EXODUS
CAPTURING VOICES
MINKA AND MARGARET
WITHIN A YARD OF HELL
THE MIDNIGHT PATROL
A LONDON SPARROW
FIREBRAND OF FLANDERS
FAITH BY HEARING
PROVING GOD
MATCHED WITH HIS HOUR
DAWN BEYOND THE ANDES
GOD'S ADVENTURER
CLIMBING ON TRACK
NO BRONZE STATUE
DESERT PILGRIM
BEATEN GOLD
AFLAME FOR CHRIST
THERE CAME A DAY
THEY SEEK A CITY
OUR RESOURCES
COUNTDOWN FOR PETER
EIGHT OF GOD'S AGENTS
BIBLE CONVOY

Books for children

TEACHER JO LIKES LITTLE CATS
KING OF THE LISU

Madame Guyon

Martyr of the Holy Spirit

by

Phyllis Thompson

HODDER AND STOUGHTON
LONDON SYDNEY AUCKLAND TORONTO

British Library Cataloguing in Publication Data
Thompson, Phyllis, *1906–*
 Madame Guyon : martyr of the Holy Spirit.
 —(Hodder Christian paperbacks)
 1. Guyon, Jeanne Marie Bouvier de la Motte
 2. Catholics—France—Biography
 3. Quietism—History
 I. Title
 248.2′2′0924   BX4705.G8

 ISBN 0 340 40175 3

Hodder and Stoughton Editorial Office: 47 Bedford Square, London WC1B 3DP.

Acknowledgements

My thanks are due to Mrs Stanley Rowe, the Rev. Paul Bassett and to all those who have encouraged me in the writing of this book, especially Miss Stephanie Wright of the Evangelical Library. Also to Miss Mollie Robertson for typing the manuscript so meticulously, and the Dr. Jonathan Chao of the Chinese Church Research Centre for permission to use the poem at the end of the Epilogue.

Contents

Prologue   9

1. The Irrevocable Step   15

2. Start of the Pilgrimage   25

3. Vanity   37

4. Dark Night Ended   51

5. Into the Unknown   73

6. Thonon to Turin   89

7. Exodus from Grenoble   99

8. Imprisoned in Paris   119

9. Enter Fenelon   133

10. Pilloried   143

11. To the Bastille   157

12. It does not end here   173

Epilogue   189

He made me understand the He did not call me, as had been thought, to the propagation of the external of the Church, which consists in winning heretics, but to the propagation of His Spirit, which is no other than the interior Spirit, and that it would be for this Spirit I would suffer.

He does not even destine me for the first conversion of sinners, but to introduce those who are already touched with the desire of being converted, into perfect conversion, which is none other than this interior Spirit.

Jeanne de la Mothe Guyon

Prologue

It was T. C. Upham who set me thinking. I'd never heard of
Madame Guyon until I read his book about her. If it had not
been given to me with a personal inscription in the flyleaf by
a young woman dying of TB, I doubt whether I should have
got any further than the title page. *Life, Religious Opinions and
Experience of Madame Guyon* held little appeal, and the opening
sentence would have put me off altogether.

'The subject of this Memoir was born on April 13th, 1648,
and baptized on the May 24th.'

1648 – three hundred years ago! But the book had been
given to me in touching circumstances, so I read on, and the
more I read, the more relevant I found it to be. The outward
conditions of that young aristocrat living in the glittering
reign of the Sun-King, Louis XIV, were vastly different from
those of myself, a rather humdrum missionary on furlough
from China, but the inner experiences had a significance I
could not ignore. True, some of them were quite beyond me,
but if I could not understand them all, or the writer's
interpretation of them, two spiritual principles emerged
which I never forgot.

One was accepting the will of God in the vicissitudes of life,
and the other the necessity of dying to self.

The processes by which they were worked out in Madame
Guyon's life were instructive and challenging when applied
personally. And I have since discovered that I am not alone
in finding them so. 'Madame Guyon! She's my favourite
character!' said one friend enthusiastically, adding more
quietly, 'Mine weren't the same as hers, of course, but I
could relate to her sufferings.'

'She helped me more than anything else in a situation in
South America in which I found myself trapped,' reflected
another. She did not go into details. Some experiences are too

personal to be shared, but, 'It was like being in prison and what she had written when she was actually there was what spoke to me – especially that little poem about a bird in a cage, singing . . .'

'Madame Guyon?' exclaimed a Canadian visitor when I mentioned her. 'Why, she was a compulsory study in the Prairie Bible Institute when I was there. L. E. Maxwell, the founder, wanted all his students to know the reality of her teaching on death to self.'

'Death to self – we don't hear much about that in these days, our minister says,' remarked an old friend, living now in Leicester. 'He's always quoting Madame Guyon . . .' He had been introduced to her when reading Dr. A. W. Tozer's biography. She was more widely known than I had realised.

Then someone reminded me that her story was the last book Watchman Nee produced before the Communists gained complete control in China. Mary Wang, Director of the China Overseas Christian Mission, had been greatly moved by it at that time, and told me, 'It was her willingness to suffer that so inspired and challenged us young people in those days.' She herself had eventually escaped from China, but most of those young people had had to remain, and it meant suffering if they were to remain loyal to Christ. The Frenchwoman who had lived three hundred years before had nerved those young Chinese Christians for what lay ahead of them in the grim second half of the twentieth century.

Madame Guyon evidently ranked among those who, being dead, continue to speak, for the message she proclaimed does not alter with the times.

Someone in the 1970s suggested that I might write her biography for the present generation, and the idea held a strong appeal, but it was not until early in 1985 that I signed a contract to do it, and set about my research. The book by T. C. Upham was all I had to go on, and I realised that he had interpreted her from his own point of view, all but making a Protestant of her. Although it had inspired me, it was an insufficient source from which to obtain as unbiased

an account of her life and character as possible, seeing she
had lived so long ago. References made to her in historical
books were sketchy and mainly derogatory, depicting her as
a rather silly religious fanatic, not clever enough to be really
dangerous, but attractive enough to be disturbing, who
made a short-lived appearance on the stage of world history.
I was not likely to glean much from them.

Then I applied for help to the Evangelical Library, and in
their archives was found just what I needed. Not only had
they *Bossuet* by H. L. Sidney Lear, *The Archbishop and the Lady*
by Michael de la Bedayère, a booklet by Mrs. Jessie Penn
Lewis, and three devotional books by Madame Guyon
herself. *A Short Method of Prayer, Spiritual Torrents* and a little
book of poems. But they had something else, which far
exceeded them all in value for my purpose. There before me
was *The Autobiography of Madame Guyon*, fully translated from
the French by Thomas Taylor Allen of the Bengal Civil
Service, and published by a firm in Charing Cross Road in
1898.

Mr. Allen made it quite plain in his preface that he took a
very dim view of 'Upham's defective and misleading *Life*,
where her catholic spirit appears bound in the grave clothes
of so-called Evangelical dogma'. As for himself, he had
translated Madame Guyon's autobiography word for word
from the French, omitting nothing. Let it speak for itself.

What better source for a biographer than the subject's own
life story as related by herself? I plunged into it with
enthusiasm and expectancy – and found myself again and
again quite out of my depth as I tried to follow the thread
of narrative in the welter of words that flowed from the pen
of a mystic. Madame Guyon wrote impulsively, just as
she saw and felt things, with very little thought as to what it
would all convey to the reader. In fact, the earlier part of
the autobiography was written on the understanding that it
would never be published at all. It was intended only for the
eye of her spiritual director, at whose command she wrote it.
The latter part was more evidently written with the view of

vindicating not only herself but others who were connected
with her. But whatever was her motive for writing, the
subject matter remained the same. With her introspective
nature she could not refrain from relating her 'religious
opinions and experience' and they sometimes made heavy
reading, especially as they were couched in the archaic
language of a former generation. But through them all
certain facts emerged which surprised me.

One was that the Bible was evidently accessible, at any
rate to the educated classes, in the reign of Louis XIV.
Madame Guyon's autobiography throughout is permeated
with Scriptural references, and she wrote and had published
commentaries on some of the Old Testament books. To
whatever extent it has been suppressed in other places and
ages, there is no suggestion that it was forbidden reading to
her and her contemporaries.

Another fact that emerged was that she was not without
friends who were willing to stand by her even when she was
most decried. She sometimes referred desperately to being
'abandoned by all', but it was an exaggeration unsupported
by evidence. One of the moving things about her story is
the loyalty displayed, not only by her to her friends, but by
her friends to her. They were impelled by the same Spirit
towards the same end – perfect union with God Himself.

And this leads to the supreme theme of Madame Guyon's
story, which is none other than the effect of the activity of the
Holy Spirit in the depths of a human soul, and a very
complex human soul at that. The effect was two-fold. On the
one hand there was the devastating revelation of the iniquity
within, the SELF which she saw and loathed, which writhed
under the blows showered upon it, but which she agreed had
to die. On the other hand there was the ineffable peace and
joy brought by the indwelling presence of God, and an
increasing knowledge, not only of the Man, Christ Jesus, but
of the power of His resurrection, and the fellowship of His
sufferings – those sufferings which because of her love for
Him, she longed to share.

It is the story of an inner life, lived in the context of circumstances very different from those of the twentieth century, and as such it can only be told with the imperfection of the writer's own limitations. But it is a story which does not end with her death. The thread of apparently incidental events which links it with the present day was so tenuous at times that the marvel is that it did not snap, yet the fact remains that her autobiography and some of her writings are still being produced in various forms today. As she herself predicted when she wrote in her prison cell, 'I have confidence that, in spite of the tempest and the storm, all You have made me say or write will be preserved.'

To trace her story, as best I can, has been a fascinating and enriching task, taking me back in time to the mid-seventeenth century, to the town of Montargis, south of Paris, where a teenage girl had just been married . . .

By sufferings only can we know
   The nature of the life we live;
The trial of our souls, they show,
   How true, how pure, the love we give.
To leave my love in doubt would be
No less disgrace than misery.

I welcome, then, with heart sincere,
   The cross my Saviour bids me take;
No load, no trial is severe,
   That's borne or suffered for His sake:
And thus my sorrow shall proclaim
A love that's worthy of the name.

Jeanne de la Mothe Guyon, aged nineteen

1

The Irrevocable Step

The young bride was in tears. It was the day after her wedding, when the pageantry and the music and the crowds of fashionable guests had carried her through the solemn ceremony in which she and the man beside her had been pronounced man and wife. Even then a sense of foreboding had robbed the occasion of the gratification she would otherwise have experienced at knowing herself to be the most beautiful bride of the season. As it was, she had found it hard to retain her poise, to smile back brightly at everyone who nodded or spoke to her. But now, the day after, when the realisation of the irrevocable step taken had dawned on her, she could control her dismay no longer. Jeanne de la Mothe had become Madame Guyon, and there was no going back on it.

It was not that her husband had treated her roughly, or that her natural modesty had been unduly affronted. It was not because the marriage had been arranged by her parents without even consulting her. That, after all, was quite customary, though she had been a little surprised when she discovered that she had signed the articles of marriage without even being told what they were. When she had met her fiancé for the first time, only three days before the wedding, she had felt he compared very unfavourably in appearance with one or two of her other suitors. In the eyes of a teenager who had been feeding her mind on romantic novels, his great wealth and good reputation scarcely compensated for his being twenty years her senior and not particularly good-looking. But the reason for her tears lay deeper than a merely natural reaction. Her desperate answer to the question, 'Whatever are you crying about?' summed up the inner conflict of her young life, for there had been times when she had seriously decided to take the veil, to be wholly dedicated to God. And now –

'Oh, I had once so desired to be a nun! Why am I married? How has this happened to me?' She had gone back on her secret vow, and now it was too late.

This pious desire had been born in her early, for from the age of two-and-a-half the greater part of her life had been spent in convents. Both her parents had been married before, already had older children, including a daughter apiece, and her mother in particular had little inclination for looking after a small girl. She preferred boys. The easy way out was to put her in the charge of the nuns whose job it was in life to look after other people's children. So to the convent of the Ursulines little Jeanne de la Mothe was sent, and there is no doubt but that she was better off with them than she was at home. The determination to be a nun was conceived in her through their example, and being of an ardent nature, on hearing some of the stories of martyrs, she asserted her willingness to become one, too. Thus early in life her sights were set on sacrifice.

It is quite probable that some of the nuns took her seriously, but schoolgirls in convents being not so very different from schoolgirls elsewhere, a few of the older girls decided to play a practical joke on this devout child.

Was she really willing to be a martyr? They would put her to the test. So one day they approached her with the solemn announcement that the time had come. God was calling her to forfeit her life for His sake. They would give her time for her last prayers, then lead her away to her execution.

On the whole Jeanne did very well. Firmly believing that her last hour had come, she knelt in prayer, then unquestioningly followed her executioners to the room they had prepared for the occasion, where a white cloth was spread on the floor to receive the blood that would be shed when her head was chopped off. But when she got there and saw one of the girls with a cutlass, with which the deed was apparently to be done, her courage failed her.

But not her pride. Unwilling to admit she feared to die, she avoided doing so by announcing with a resourcefulness unusual in one so young, that she could not be a martyr yet, since she had not asked her father's permission. Without that, it would not be right to proceed.

The howl of derisive laughter that greeted this explanation no doubt had an element of relief in it, for the jokers were fast approaching the point where they themselves would have been compelled to give up. But for Jeanne the sense of humiliation was not only that she had failed in the eyes of her companions, nor was it only that she had let herself down. There was the uneasy fear that she had come short in the eyes of God, and was no longer in His favour. That unseen Being of whom she was daily reminded in the religious services in the convent set very high standards . . .

Her failure as a martyr worried her more than the lies she told quite fluently, which could be duly disposed of in the confessional box.

All the same, she was happy while with the nuns, most of whom treated her very kindly. In the convent she was spared the peculiar grief experienced by a child at home who knows herself to be the one unloved. Her brother, not she, was their mother's favourite. He, it seemed, could do no wrong, while she could do nothing right. He was indulged, she was reprimanded. If he wanted something of hers, it was taken from her and given to him. Her childish efforts to win approval, to do something that would bring a smile to her mother's face, and a kiss and a hug, were in vain. A cold look of disapproval greeted her instead.

Her happiest times were when she was in the Ursuline convent where her paternal half-sister, who really loved her, was put in charge of her. 'Oh, I enjoy teaching you more than doing anything else!' exclaimed the young nun one day. She spent every spare moment allowed her with her little sister. Under her tuition the child developed well, with charming manners and a ready wit which so attracted the exiled Queen of England, widow of Charles the First, that she wanted to adopt her. She was staying in the de la Mothe home at the time, and Jeanne had been brought back on a visit.

'Let her come to me. I'll train her as Maid of Honour to the Princess,' she said. But Jeanne's elderly father, who was very fond of his little daughter, though he did not often see her, refused to part with her. For various reasons, however, he was persuaded to remove her from the convent of the Ursulines and place her in one of another order – the Dominicans this time. And it was here that she found the Vulgate version of the Bible.

How it came about that the book had been left in the little room allotted to her is a mystery, but there it was, and as she was quite often ill and confined to bed, she had ample opportunity to read it.

She was fascinated. At that age it was naturally the narratives that appealed to her most, and being alone for hours on end – when she was ill, she learned many of them off by heart.

'I spent whole days in reading it,' she wrote in her autobiography years later. 'And having great powers of recollection I committed to memory the historical parts entirely.' The self-imposed task occupied her mind and gave her vivid imagination the opportunity to reach out far beyond the restricted world in which she lived. Abraham the nomad with the flocks and his herds, Joseph sold by his brothers into slavery, Moses defying Pharaoh in the name of the God of Israel, David hounded by the jealousy of Saul – she knew them all, and felt herself at one with them. Her familiarity with the Scriptures, which revealed itself later in so many of her writings (she produced commentaries on the whole Bible at one stage) had its roots in those lonely hours as a child in a sick room in a Dominican convent.

Nor was the Bible the only book she read during those impressionable years of her disrupted and rather unhappy childhood. The writings of St. John of the Cross and other Christian mystics appealed to her. Particularly what she

read of St. Francis de Sales and Madame du Chantal
influenced her thinking.

It was these two, whose lives had been so strangely
entwined in a mystical union, who attracted her most. After
all, it was less than a hundred years ago that they had lived
and laboured in the north of the country, not far from
Geneva, that hot-bed of Calvinism. It was claimed that St.
Francis had converted thousands of Protestants back to the
Church of Rome, sometimes, it was inferred, at the risk of his
life, in addition to founding with Madame du Chantal the
Order of the Visitation. Scores of communities had been
established, and their black-robed nuns were a common
sight on errands of mercy to the poor.

The practical achievements of Francis de Sales and
Madame du Chantal were matched by the spiritual quality
of their lives. Their love for God, their teaching on the will of
God and the crucifixion of the self-life had been duly
examined and pronounced pure by the hierarchy in Rome.
What they had written could therefore be relied on, and the
ten-year-old girl, perusing their books, discovered something
new.

She learned that they prayed.

This secret activity of theirs awakened within her a vague
awareness of a realm about which she knew nothing. Their
prayer was apparently different from the incantations and
recitals, the versicles and responses, to which she was
accustomed. It went much deeper. She wished she could
pray, and made some attempts to do so, without any
apparent result. But desire had been born, a conscious
vacuum waiting to be filled

So passed the earlier years of her life, with fluctuating
aspirations after higher things which were largely condi-
tioned by her circumstances, by the examples she admired,
and by the books which she read.

The influence of those books, read in the impressionable
years of her childhood, was incalculable. Because she was
often alone, her imagination had freedom to stretch out and

expand, and the writers of the books became as real to her as the people she met in ordinary life. Madame du Chantal was her heroine. 'All the vows she made, I made also, as aiming always at the perfect, and doing the will of God in all things.' Reading that in her ardour Madame du Chantal had branded the name of Jesus on her breast with a red hot iron, she wished she could do the same. 'Jesus.' That was the name Madame du Chantal had chosen, not Mary or one of the saints. How could she, a little girl in a convent, obtain the necessary means to brand the name on her own skin? Eventually she had to give up that idea, but decided on the next best thing. She would write the name carefully on a piece of paper, then pin it to her skin. It must have been a very painful operation, but she went through with it, and 'it continued for a long time fixed in this manner'.

'My only thought was to become a nun, and I went very often to the Visitation to beg them to be willing to receive me, for the love I had for St. Francis de Sales did not allow me to think of other convents.' The mystical union between St. Francis de Sales and Madame du Chantal, joint founders of the Order, she accepted without question. They were knit together by a spiritual, not a natural affinity, altogether in keeping with the religious life they had chosen. It was the only sort of union that made any appeal to her.

However, this excess of ardent piety later swung to the opposite extreme. As she entered her teens it was romantic novels, not the writings of the mystics, that kept her reading into the early hours of the morning. Her own reflection in the mirror, viewed from as many angles as possible, gave her a much more animated and attractive object of adoration than the image of the Virgin Mary. In her mirror she saw a beautiful girl, with lustrous eyes and a flawless fair skin, soft curls and a well-formed mouth. Much prettier, she knew, than most of the other girls and young women in the social circles of Montargis, and she thought with secret scorn of their defects, although she was careful never to reveal it. Jeanne de la Mothe had a charmingly modest manner which enhanced her still further in the eyes of her admirers – of whom she herself was the most fervent. When she went out she was, of course, always accompanied by her mother or a chaperone, but that did not deter her from noticing the glances of warm admiration in her direction from members of the opposite sex – nor of envious dislike from her own! She was equally gratified by both.

Nevertheless: 'I did not fail every day to say my vocal prayers, to make confession pretty often, and to communicate almost every fortnight. I was sometimes in church weeping and praying to the Holy Virgin to obtain my conversion . . . I was very charitable. I loved the poor.' In this her mother had set her a good example, for Madame de la Mothe was very generous to needy people in her neighbourhood, as her daughter readily admitted.

Then, when she was in her mid-teens, her parents took her to Paris.

Paris! Capital of the nation fast becoming the greatest power in western Europe, centre of art and culture, fashion and frivolity. Paris with its boulevards and its magnificent buildings, the Louvre and Notre Dame, its bridges over the Seine, its tall, sharp-roofed houses with their diamond-paned mullion windows and little iron balconies. Paris with its elegantly dressed ladies bowing and smiling from sedan chairs on the chivalrous gentlemen in their richly embroidered cloaks who swept off their hats with a flourish and bowed low in homage. Paris with its animated visitors in the salons, its fêtes and its hunting parties led by the virile young King, glad to be in the saddle with his mistress beside him after hours at his desk studying reports.

Paris with its preachers, too. If the King had made adultery the fashion, he also set the example of outward piety, attending Mass regularly and listening with apparent approval to the forthright sermons of men like Bossuet, who pulled no punches, even in the presence of His Majesty. There were few public entertainments in the seventeenth century, and eloquent preachers could always draw a crowd.

The confessional boxes provided a different sort of outlet, where those who were uneasy about their souls could acknowledge their sins and misdemeanours with the assurance that the priest behind the grill was pledged to secrecy, and would not betray their confidences. To go to Mass, to go to confession, to observe the feast days of the saints, was all part of the fashionable round, and in addition it was quite the right thing to have your own personal spiritual director, who gave you good advice, writing letters on occasion to point out your faults, making suggestions for your spiritual improvement, and generally taking an interest in you.

Religion was something to be donned and doffed, as occasion served, but not to be taken too seriously, except by those who were called to it, and saw it as their vocation. Or, in some cases, as the only way out. To women it was the one alternative to marriage – that is, to the women born into the fortunate ten per cent of French families who lived in affluence; the aristocrats, the nobility, the wealthy landowners. The remaining ninety per cent, including the indiscriminate rabble responsible for the Bread Riots, were of course in an entirely different category, about which the ten per cent knew very little, except that those who happened to live near enough to them provided objects of charity to whom gifts of food and clothing and money could be given from time to time. Charity was a Christian virtue to be cultivated, as it offset failings in other directions.

Jeanne de la Mothe belonged to the privileged ten per cent, and as she was developing into a very attractive girl, with every prospect of making a good match, her parents saw no reason for her to take the veil.

Neither, at this time, did she.

What she saw of life in Paris, the gaiety and the intellectual pursuits, the lavish entertaining and the elegance, delighted her. This was what she wanted – the opportunity to display her charm and her beauty, 'to make myself loved without loving anybody', and to be free from the domination of her mother. Marriage, it seemed, would be the open door to the gratification of all these desires. She began to have her doubts when she learned to whom she had been affianced and realised that his wealth rather than his rank was the attraction in her father's eyes, and the fact that he spent most of his time in her own home town, Montargis, and would not be likely to take her to live far away, or abroad. As the time drew near for the wedding there was also the natural shrinking from the unknown mysteries of the bed, to be shared with a strange man. But it was not until the wedding day itself that the oppressive cloud descended so heavily on her spirit that she could not eat. She had a presentiment then that she was entering gloom, not brightness, and the presentiment proved to be true. The full realisation of it broke when her husband took her back to Montargis, to the home where his mother was in unchallenged control. Her own mother's attitude had been strangely lacking in love, but now she was to be plunged into an atmosphere of suppressed hostility.

My husband was reasonable and loved me. When I was ill he was inconsolable to a surprising degree, and yet he did not cease to get into passions with me. I believe that, but for his mother and that maid of whom I have spoken, I should have been very happy with him; for as to hastiness, there is hardly a man who has not plenty of it, and it is the duty of a reasonable woman to put up with it quietly without increasing it by sharp answers.

You made use of all these things, O my God, for my salvation. Through Your goodness You have so managed things that I have afterwards seen this course was absolutely necessary for me, in order to make me die to my vain and haughty natural character . . . an altogether wise dispensation of Your providence.

Jeanne de la Mothe Guyon, in her autobiography.

2

Start of the Pilgrimage

'I was no sooner at home with my new husband than I saw clearly it would be to me a house of sorrow,' she recorded in her autobiography years later, and so it proved to be. Her mother-in-law was an austere, uncultured woman, and one in whom thrift had become such an obsession as to make life a misery. The young Madame Guyon, whose parents were not nearly so wealthy as the family into which she had married, found herself in a dark, heavily furnished home which lacked all the brightness and elegance to which she had become accustomed. Gone was the atmosphere of refinement and culture, the intelligent discussions and the witty sallies, the hum of conversation and the chuckles of laughter, the music and the colour of the salons of Paris. The upbringing and temperament of Madame Guyon senior precluded such frivolities, and she would have none of them.

What was worse, from the point of view of the newly arrived young mistress of the home, was that the manners of the household were different. If her own mother had chided her unduly when she was a child, she had treated her with courtesy in the presence of others as she grew older, while her father, pleased to see his attractive young daughter cultivating charming manners and obviously delighting the guests who came frequently to their home, had encouraged her to join in their conversations and express her opinions.

Now all that was changed. The natural charm that had been one of her greatest assets was repulsed. She was no longer a centre of admiration, moving easily among those whose interest and approval brought out all her social graces. Her mother-in-law, it soon became evident, resented her presence, was angered by her refinement, and suspected her motives. The young girl's cultured voice and polished manners were in sharp contrast to her own rather uncouth ways, putting her at a disadvantage against which she fought angrily.

Right from the start young Madame Guyon realised that there was no doubt as to who reigned supreme in the Guyon household. The hopes she had entertained of freedom to reign as mistress in her own home were dashed completely. The cooks and the coachmen, the maids, the valets and the footmen, even her husband himself, were under control of the older Madame. Her own position was virtually that of a captive, and a despised one at that. She was accustomed to being accompanied by a maid or a footman when she went out, and they had been with her to protect her from embarrassments, and generally ease things for her. She very soon found that the maid or the footman who now went with her was expected to report when they got home on everything she had done, and everyone she had spoken to. There was a subtle difference in their attitude towards her, too. They knew it was the old Madame who held the reins, not the newly-arrived young bride, and that to win favour with the one, the other could be slighted. One maid in particular, who was in the confidence of her mother-in-law, was quite insolent, and the teenage girl scarcely knew how to control her indignation. On a few occasions she flared up, but that only made matters worse. Her mother-in-law sided with the maid.

It would not have been so bad if at least in the presence of guests and relatives her mother-in-law had shown a semblance of respect towards her, but she did not. If she entered into a discussion at the table or in the salon, she was snubbed. If she remained silent, she was accused of being sulky.

'She spoke disparagingly of me to everyone, hoping thereby to diminish the esteem and affection each had for me, so that she put insults upon me in the presence of the best society.' She longed for someone in whom she could confide her distress, someone who would comfort her and give her some moral support, but the one person to whom she could have poured out her sorrows without fear of being misunderstood, her half-sister the Ursuline nun, had just died. When others spoke to her own mother about the indignities she suffered she was reprimanded sharply for being so poor-spirited as to put up with it.

'You forget your rank!' she was told. 'You should not allow yourself to be spoken to like that. Nor should you allow your social inferiors to be placed above you at table and in the salon. That a de la Mothe should give precedence to such persons! Have you forgotten that your father is Seigneur of Montargis?'

Young Madame Guyon, so eager to please everyone, found she could please no one. Even her husband, who was very fond of her in his way, did little to defend her. He was almost completely under the influence of his mother and the maid in her confidence, who, being a good nurse, was the one who tended him when he was ill. And as it soon appeared, the man had his own troubles, one of which came to light four months after the marriage.

He had developed gout.

Now gout, with the limited medical remedies available in the seventeenth century, could be a very painful disease, and in its way rather humiliating into the bargain. The unfortunate Monsieur Guyon took to his bed with it for weeks on end, during which time his young wife waited on him assiduously. For this she got into trouble with her mother. 'You are very foolish to spend so much time with him,' she was told. 'You are laying up trouble for yourself. What you are doing out of kindness he will take for granted, and you'll find yourself more and more tied to him, and get no thanks for it.' Then she complained that her daughter never came to see her own parents, and had obviously ceased to love them.

Her friends argued with her, too. 'A girl of your age to be wasting your talents, nursing a sick man! It's disgraceful.'

'As I have a husband, I ought to share his troubles as well as his wealth,' she answered mildly. There was a stoical streak in her nature, and she always managed to put on a brave face, however she was feeling. They might have thought her very happy with her husband if it had not been for the bad temper he sometimes showed towards her, even in the presence of others. She was determined to be dutiful, and on the occasions when he was evidently appreciative of her presence she was relieved, even satisfied. More often, however, he was thoroughly irritable, and what with the fault-finding of her mother-in-law, and the unrestrained insolence of the maid-servant, she became so cowed outwardly and so desperate inwardly that she was in despair.

One day, all her efforts to say the right thing having been snubbed or ridiculed or indignantly repudiated, she escaped to her room in such an overwrought state that she had to do something to give vent to her feelings. An extrovert would have screamed, lashed out, smashed some furniture, but it was typical of Madame Guyon that she turned in on herself. Grasping a sharp knife she thought wildly, 'I'll cut out my tongue! Then I shan't be able to speak, I shan't be able to say the wrong thing. I'll cut out my tongue!' Reason triumphed over the madness of the moment, and she did not do it, but the thought of becoming dumb persisted, and she prayed constantly that she might lose the power of speech. 'I even communicated and had Masses said that I might become dumb, such a child was I still.'

The effect of this daily hostility from which she could rarely escape, for she was required to spend all her time in her mother-in-law's apartment, was to crush her vivacity and drive her into silence. Before her marriage she had been an animated girl, with exceptional conversational powers and a ready wit. Now she was quiet, timid, with nothing to say for herself. She seemed almost stupid, and was certainly very unhappy. What made things worse for her was the remembrance of two or three of the young men who had sought her hand in marriage earlier. Young, charming, well-bred – how much happier she would have been had a marriage been arranged with one of them!

But it was the very misery of the circumstances in which she found herself that forced her back to God.

'These severe crosses made me return to you, O my God. I commenced to deplore the sins of my youth . . .

'I endeavoured to improve my life by penitence and a general confession . . .

'I gave up at once all romantic novels, although they were at one time my passion . . . though it had weakened some time before my marriage by the reading of the Gospel . . . I found it so beautiful, and I discovered in it a character of truth that disgusted me with all other books . . .

'I resumed prayer, and I endeavoured not to offend you, O my God. I felt that little by little your love was regaining the supremacy in my heart.'

Suffering was the pathway leading her to God.

*   *   *

'While you are brushing my hair I'll read aloud from this book,' said young Madame Guyon pleasantly to the maid who was standing, brush in hand, behind her. 'It's by St. Francis de Sales, and it's called *An Introduction to the Devout Life*. It is written for people in all walks of life, and it shows us how we can all be devout, whatever our circumstances. I've got to the part about mental prayer,' and picking up the book she started to read.

' "Perhaps you do not know how to pray mentally – that is, in your heart. Unfortunately, this is a thing that few in our age know how to do. For this reason, I give you a short and plain method" . . . Oh!' She gave an involuntary exclamation of pain as the maid brushing her hair pulled at it too hard, but quickly resumed her reading. She wanted her maid to profit by what she was reading, as well as herself, even though she really did not understand what was written.

' "Place yourself in His sacred presence. Reflect that God is not only in the place in which you are, but that He is, in a most particular manner, in your heart, and in the very

centre of your being . . . Heart of your heart. Spirit of your
spirit. . . !" '

In years to come she was to use almost exactly the same
words when she set out to teach people how to pray. They
were sown in the fertile soil of her mind, though the time had
not yet come when she would know their reality. These
writings of St. Francis de Sales attracted her because they
were intended, not only for monks and nuns and those whose
lives could be so ordered as to put devotional exercises first,
but for people in the workaday world where the claims of
home and employment left little time for such occupations.
What she read aroused desire for what St. Francis evidently
possessed, and in order to obtain it she decided it was
necessary to be a devout person. For this reason she had
resolved to pray twice every day, to go frequently to
confession, and to check carefully on her faults. How that
vanity of hers asserted and reasserted itself! She deliberately
had her hair dressed very simply, refrained from looking in
the mirror, and tried to think of something else when she
went out, but try as she would she could not help being
gratified by the glances cast in her direction which told
her that she looked very, very pretty. Even in church she
was conscious of her attractive appearance, thinking more
about it than about the prayers and the responses and all that
ought to have been absorbing her mind. She wrote these and
other failings honestly in a book, going over the records each
week to see how well she was succeeding in eliminating
them.

'Alas! This labour, though tiring, was of but little use,
because I trusted in my own efforts. I wished, indeed, to be
reformed, but my good desires were weak and languid.'

All the same, as time went on, there was some improvement, and on the practical side she developed a virtue
which had been set by her own mother, who had recently
died. She had been particularly charitable to the poor, so
now young Madame Guyon, following her example, went
personally to visit the poor in her own neighbourhood, to

give them material help when necessary, and to do something to alleviate their sufferings when ill. She had been an
intelligent child with an interest in medicine and in the
course of her sojourns in various convents besides picking up
simple remedies for common complaints, had learned to
compound some very effective ointments. She began putting
some of her skills into practice, and her happiest hours were
those employed in this way.

It was not only the useful employment that satisfied her.
Such meritorious acts also provided her with practically the
only reason whereby she could escape the confinement of the
house and her mother-in-law's criticisms. There were,
however, occasions when she was able to visit her father, to
whom she was devoted, although she stood somewhat in awe
of him. It was through him that she was brought in touch
with three people who played a decisive part in her spiritual
pilgrimage at that time.

The first was the Duchess of Charost, whose father, a
prominent court official, had been imprisoned by the King,
so his daughter, temporarily in exile, had found a refuge in
the de la Mothe household. Young Madame Guyon, on
meeting her, had been impressed by the tranquil expression
on her face, and also by her readiness to talk about prayer
and the inner life and God, the God of whom St. Francis de
Sales wrote so intimately.

'I want to please God,' Madame Guyon confided simply to
this new friend, and related some of her efforts to do so, to
which she received a rather perplexing reply.

'Yes, I can see you live a bustling, active sort of life,' said
the Duchess of Charost. 'That is good. But your prayer life
seems very complicated. For me, prayer is much simpler.'

Much simpler, and much more satisfying, Madame
Guyon reflected, and wondered why there was such a
difference. She looked with admiration at the beatific
appearance of the Duchess of Charost's face, and tried to
emulate it, tried to cultivate an inner composure which
would result in an equally peaceful expression.

Inner composure, in her case, took the form of resignation at best, and a bottled-up rebellion at worst, neither of which is conducive to genuine tranquillity.

There was something else about the Duchess of Charost's demeanour, however, which quickened her interest and curiosity. It was revealed when Monsieur de Chamesson, a nephew of de la Mothe, returned from Cochin China, and paid a visit to his uncle.

Monsieur de Chamesson had gone to Cochin China as a missionary, some years before, and Madame Guyon, as a child, had heard about him and his reputation for zeal and piety. She had wept bitterly because, when he passed through Montargis on his way to Cochin China, she had not seen him. Now that he had returned she was thrilled to be able to meet him, and was touched at his evident concern for her, his ardent young cousin. But what impressed her more than anything else was the way in which he and Madame de Charost seemed to understand each other right from the start. They had never met before, but within minutes of being introduced they were talking with the unihibited intimacy of those who have known each other for a very long time, and are held together by a strong mutual attachment. Madame Guyon had never seen anything quite like it before, and she knew instinctively what was that invisible bond of union.

They both loved God. Devout Roman Catholics as they were, they were punctilious in their observance of various acts of piety, attending Mass and confession, fasts and feasts, but she knew that their inner satisfaction was rooted in something deeper than outward rites could provide. They tried to help her to understand, to teach her a simpler form of prayer. When her cousin told her that there were times at prayer when he thought of nothing, she was mystified. Silent communion of man's spirit with God was beyond her. She depended on her own mental activities, forcing herself to meditate on some aspect of God's goodness or Christ's sacrifice, uttering ejaculations and repeating prayers when alone, bemoaning her shortcomings and castigating herself for her sinful tendencies.

And she seemed to be getting nowhere. The efforts of her two friends to enlighten her were apparently useless. As she herself observed later, their prayers were more efficacious than their words, and prepared the way for the divine moment in which the revelation of what she was blindly seeking came to her. The fullness of time had come for her at last.

Years later she wrote of it in the words, 'O, my divine Love, the desire I had to please You, the tears I shed, my great labours and the little fruit I reaped from it, moved Your compassion. You gave me in a moment, through Your grace and through Your goodness alone, what I had been unable to give myself through all my efforts.'

The revelation came to her through the lips of a Franciscan monk who, after living in solitude for five years, had recently come to the neighbourhood of Montargis with a deep conviction that God had something important for him to do there. The idea in his own mind was that it would lead to the conversion of an influential man in the neighbourhood, but as a matter of fact, nothing came of his efforts in that direction. He little thought that the object of his mission might be a girl in her teens. Such an idea never entered his head. Had he not vowed that he would avoid women altogether, unless God very clearly showed him otherwise? And since he had received no special intimation that such a thing might happen, on the day when he saw two women approaching him, one a singularly beautiful, fashionably dressed young woman, he wondered if he were dreaming. And when she started talking to him, he felt thoroughly embarrassed.

She introduced herself as the daughter of the Seigneur de la Mothe, and said that her father had sent her to him to ask his help. She was in spiritual difficulty. She could not pray as she ought. She tried to concentrate, but her mind wandered. Her vanity, her many faults, hindered her devotion. She tried to live always in the presence of God, this was her aim, but she could not achieve it. She went frequently to confession, to Mass, observed all the ordinances, repeated prayers, did everything she knew, but still she could not find what she wanted – the continual presence of God. What must she do?

The Franciscan monk was silent, so she went on talking, trying to explain her difficulty, feeling that she was not making herself intelligible to him. His quietness slightly disturbed her, and the fact that apart from the elderly woman she had brought as a chaperone, she was alone with a man. She was a very circumspect young woman, determined that on no account would she give occasion for gossip or scandal. Indeed, had it not been that her father, to whom she had confided her spiritual longings, had urged her to seek the Franciscan's help, she would not have come to him. And now that she had come, he seemed to have nothing to say.

Had she but realised it, he himself was at a loss to know what to do. Not having spoken to a woman for five years, he would gladly have escaped from what he felt was a potentially inflammable situation, but there was no way out. Her questionings demanded an answer, and gradually it dawned on him that behind that dangerously attractive exterior was a soul seeking desperately to find God. And God was so very, very near! All that was necessary was to tell her so.

'Madame, it is because you seek outside what you have within,' the monk said at last. 'Accustom yourself to seek God in your heart, and you will find Him there.' And then, without another word, he left her.

The effect on the girl of those two short sentences was amazing. 'They were for me like an arrow that pierced my heart through and through. I felt in that moment a very deep wound, delicious and full of love, a wound so sweet I desired never to be healed of it.' All her life she remembered that occasion as the time of her conversion. Yet there was nothing new in what had been said. Had not St. Francis de Sales said the same thing? And had she not read in the Gospel itself 'The kingdom of God is not here and there, but the kingdom of God is within you'? She had read it without understanding it, but in that moment of revelation she saw the true meaning at last. Her heart was the kingdom over which God had come to reign. He was there. He was with her. And the effect of His presence was not to shame or terrify her, but on the contrary, to fill her with an indescribable ecstasy of love.

'Your love, O my God, was not only for me like a delightful oil, but also like a devouring fire, which kindled in my heart such a flame that it seemed bound to devour everything in an instant. I was no longer recognisable either by myself, or by others.' All consciousness of the faults that had worried her was swallowed up in the bliss of being accepted without question and loved unconditionally.

'I don't know what you've done to me,' she said excitedly to the Franciscan when she went again to see him. 'My heart is quite changed. I love God. Oh, I love Him! I love Him!'

Happy Solitude - Unhappy Men

My heart is easy, and my burden light;
I smile, though sad, when Thou art in my sight;
The more my woes in secret I deplore
I taste Thy goodness and I love the more.

There, while a solemn stillness reigns around,
Faith, Love and Hope within my soul abound;
And while the world suppose me lost in care,
The joy of angels, unperceived, I share.

Thy creatures wrong Thee, O Thou Sovereign Good:
Thou art not loved, because not understood;
This grieves me most, that vain pursuits beguile
Ungrateful men, regardless of Thy smile.

Frail beauty and false honour are adored;
While Thee they scorn, and trifle with Thy Word;
Pass, unconcern'd, a Saviour's sorrows by;
And hunt their ruin with a zeal to die.

Jeanne de la Mothe Guyon

3

Vanity

'She's under a delusion,' announced Madame Guyon's confessor, and her mother-in-law agreed. So did her husband. Her manner was most peculiar, they considered. It was not that she had become argumentative or arrogant, or that she behaved badly. She was, in fact, even more docile than she had been before going to see that Franciscan monk who had had such a strange effect on her. There had been times in the past when she had flared up in temper, especially when one of the maids had been impertinent. But now that never happened, even under severe provocation. She was not so finicky about what she ate, either. Indeed, she seemed deliberately to choose the things she had formerly disliked.

What irritated them was a change that had taken place within her which was hard to define, except that she seemed to have some secret source of satisfaction which they could not fathom. She would close her eyes and sit quietly while others were talking, and when spoken to often did not hear until shaken or addressed again sharply. Then she would open her eyes and look round almost in bewilderment before speaking, as though she had been dragged back from another world.

She herself might well have described it in that way. There was a world unseen, into which she could retreat and experience peace and joy, a world in which the love of God so enfolded her, transported her, that speech was almost impossible.

'Nothing was now more easy for me than to pray. Hours were to me no more than moments, and I was unable not to do it.' But her prayer was quite different from what she had been taught and had recited so painstakingly. It was no longer an exhausting mental activity, but rather an awareness of God's presence that was overwhelming. 'Nothing of my prayer passed into my head, but it was a prayer of enjoyment and possession of the will, where the delight of God was so great, so pure, and so simple . . . Everything was absorbed in a delicious faith, where all distinctions were lost to give love room for loving without motives or reason for loving.'

For all her unusually analytical mind, when it came to defining love, young Madame Guyon could find no words beyond those 'loving without motives or reasons for loving'. It was not the holiness and the justice, not even the love and the mercy revealed through the sacrifice of His Son, that ravished her, but God Himself. 'I love Him because I love Him,' was her simple explanation, and in her wildest imagination she could conceive of no circumstance or condition in which she would cease to love Him. Hers was essentially the religion of the heart, and this is what her enemies and detractors could never understand. They found themselves up against something which went beyond intellectual apprehension, a living force stronger than the determination of the will.

In those early days, when she was at the mercy of her husband's household, her ardent desire for silent communion with God was viewed with disapproval. They thought she was going mad, and decided to put a curb on this incessant praying. If she was absent for half an hour, and was found to be praying, she was called peremptorily away, and made to sit with her mother-in-law, or by the bedside of her husband when he was ill. The effort to concentrate on things around her, to make appropriate responses in idle conversation, was such a strain that there were times when she was incapable of acting normally. To make matters worse, there was the increasing insolence of the particular maid whose position in the Guyon household was so firmly entrenched. On one occasion the woman created such a scene, asserting that she was being badly treated by her young mistress, that Monsieur Guyon threw his crutch at his wife, and insisted that she should apologise. The principle of obedience to authority was so deeply ingrained in her that she obeyed without a moment's hesitation, although she knew she had done no wrong. She went even further. She gave the maid a present. The only effect this gentleness had on the woman was to elicit the remark, 'There you are. I knew I was in the right!' and the insolence continued.

Worst of all, perhaps, was the attitude of her eldest child towards her. The little boy was spoiled by his grandmother, and when Madame Guyon tried to correct his faults, he knew where to go for support.

'Grandma says you used to tell far worse lies that I do!' he told her defiantly when she had found him out in a falsehood. She did not deny it – lying had been one of her besetting sins, as she acknowledged.

'It's because I know how wrong it was of me to tell those lies that I want to stop you doing the same thing,' she replied, and she was grieved to see the expression of defiance on the little face. He referred to her contemptuously as 'she' sometimes when he spoke of her, she knew, and was not reprimanded for it. The attitude of her own child towards her was the hardest of all to bear, but she accepted even this as a cross that she must carry for the sake of her love for God.

Her crosses. All the afflictions and reverses of this mortal life were the crosses she was called upon to bear, and the heavier the cross, the deeper was the inner consolation, the consolation of fellowship with Christ. Had not His been a life of suffering, crowned with the crucifixion?

'. . . You taught me so well a Jesus Christ crucified, that I madly loved the cross, and all that did not bear the character of cross and suffering failed to please me.'

This love of suffering drove her to strange extremes. She scourged herself, wore girdles of hair with iron nails, lay on nettles and brambles and thorns. She put stones in her shoes, so that even walking was painful. Whether these self-inflicted penances achieved anything beyond adding to her already overwrought condition is open to doubt, but her stern handling of her natural appetites soon had a very salutary result. By abstaining from the things that she most enjoyed, and eating what was most distasteful, she completely overcame her fastidiousness, and in less than a year she could eat whatever was put before her with imperturbability.

In addition to controlling her appetite, she entered into situations which she would formerly have found intolerably revolting. Pus-filled wounds and bleeding sores would have horrified her, but now, when injured or sick people were brought into the house she personally attended to the dressings, and used ointments she had made. Her activities along this line, and in visiting and helping the poor, were evidently tolerated, even approved, by her mother-in-law, for while so employed she could obviously not be indulging in that secret passion for silent prayer. What the older woman probably did not realise was that her young daughter-in-law was gaining a reputation in the town for piety and good works. It was a reputation which was to stand her in good stead when she became the object of slander in later years.

Even at that time, however, she was becoming a controversial figure in her home town of Montargis. The treatment she received at the hands of her mother-in-law, and the patient way in which she accepted it did not pass unnoticed, and there were some who said she was a saint. On the other hand, her own confessor asserted that she had gone astray, and the monks of his order even referred to her openly as being completely deceived.

As for Madame Guyon herself, she did not know what to think. Something was happening within her which she could not understand. For instance, she had become so acutely aware of her own shortcomings that she went to church one day in order to obtain the remission of the temporal punishment due to her sins. The guilt had been dealt with, she knew, for she had confessed each one and been absolved, but the debt of temporal punishment remained, and the way to get rid of it was to obtain indulgences. She had been taught that a sort of spiritual treasury had been formed by the surplus merits of Christ, and the Virgin Mary, and all the saints, and from that treasury a sinner like herself, unable to do sufficient penance to expiate all her sin, could draw. This principle of vicarious satisfaction was one with which she had been familiar from childhood, and she accepted it without question, as she accepted all the dogmas of the church to which she belonged. But when she entered the church building that day, intent on obtaining the necessary indulgences from the priest, whatever the penance imposed required, she was so overcome by the sense of God's love, she could not do it. She wanted to take her own punishment at His hands, whatever it might be, as a child accepts its father's strokes, knowing they are merited. As the prophet Micah said, 'I will bear the indignation of the Lord, because I have sinned against Him, until He plead my cause, and execute judgment for me.' Indulgences were all very well for those souls who did not know the value of suffering, nor desire that divine justice should be satisfied; who were more afraid of the penalty that follows wrong-doing than displeasing a holy God. But as far as she was concerned, she preferred to suffer when she had done wrong.

So she obtained no indulgences that day and went home. However, not being quite sure that her attitude was right, not having heard or read of anyone else holding her views, she went along to church another day with the same object in view, but again she found she could not ask for indulgences, and gave up the idea. She wrote to the Franciscan monk, telling him what she thought about indulgences, and expressed herself with such freedom and clarity that he incorporated her words in his sermon the following day.

The matter of indulgences was not the only one which, as far as she was concerned, she felt she could dispense with.

There was the habit of praying to the Virgin Mary or St. Mary Magdalene, or one of the saints, asking for their intercession on her behalf. Somehow, she now found herself instinctively by-passing them, so to speak, and going direct to God Himself. This perplexed her. She had the utmost veneration for the saints, and for the Virgin, and all her life had been taught to invoke their aid. Why did it no longer seem necessary to do so? She eventually came to a conclusion that satisfied her. Jesus Christ was the bridegroom of her soul, and with that relationship, what need had she for the kindly intermediacy of others? It was quite logical to need their services no longer, however deeply they were to be admired and commemorated, since a bridegroom would care for the needs of his bride without being prompted by others. Having thought the matter through on these lines, she had no further compunction about not praying to the saints.

There was one thing that really worried her, however, and this was her vanity. She was not particularly aware of it in Montargis, but when she accompanied her husband to Paris for a time it flared up again, although it was apparent to no one but herself. Indeed, the priests whom she met when she went to confession were astonished that one so young and attractive should have so little of a serious character to confess, and they told her so.

'They said to me that I could not sufficiently thank God for the graces He had bestowed on me; that if I knew them I would be astonished. Some declared they did not know a woman whom God kept so close and in so great a purity of conscience.

'What made it such was that continual care you had over me, O my God, making me experience your intimate presence, as you have promised us in your Gospel, "If any one does My will, We will come unto him and make our dwelling in Him."' This she wrote in her autobiography years later, and with hindsight added the significant words, 'But alas! My dear Love, when You ceased Yourself to watch, how weak I was, and how my enemies prevailed over me. Let others attribute their victories to their own faithfulness; for me, I will only attribute them to Your paternal care. I have proved my weakness too well, and had such a fatal experience of what I should be without You, to presume anything was due to my own care.'

Her weakness, to the average person, would have seemed innocent enough. The gaiety of Paris was infectious, and it was natural that a young, beautiful woman should be affected by it. As far as she was concerned, she behaved with restraint and decorum outwardly, but inwardly found herself yielding again to that vanity of hers, with its gratification at being seen and admired, its willingness to be loved without loving in return. When she took a turn on the promenade it was as much to be looked at as for the exercise. '. . . I knew the violent passion certain persons had for me, and I allowed them to show it,' she wrote, although she was careful never to be alone with them. 'I also committed faults in leaving my neck a little uncovered, although it was not nearly so much so as others had it. I wept because I saw I was growing slack, and it was a very great torment for me.'

Since the memorable conversation with the Franciscan monk she had never been without the powerful attraction of God's love in her heart. Now that seemed weaker, and the instincts of nature were reasserting themselves. It was a time, as with King Hezekiah, when it is recorded that 'the Lord left him, that he might know what was in his heart'. The diminishing sense of God's presence was giving young Madame Guyon a practical revelation of what she would be like if left to herself, and it was very alarming. When some of her admirers arranged a special party for her at Saint Cloud, where Monsieur, the King's brother, had his residence, she accepted their invitation although very uneasy about doing so. It was a magnificent affair, with entertainments and a banquet, everything done on a lavish scale, and the guests all behaved admirably, doing and saying nothing that could give offence to the young woman who was noted for her piety. All the same, she was thoroughly miserable. She was wise enough to realise where this sort of thing could lead her, for she was not ignorant of the moral laxity of Paris at that time. Knowing that her own vanity and weakness had led her into this fashionable, extravagant set, she felt she had deeply offended God. All sense of His presence left her, and it was three months before her peace of heart was restored.

While in Paris she had a strange experience which left an indelible mark on her memory. She had decided to go to Notre Dame on foot rather than in a carriage, and accompanied by a lackey, was crossing one of the bridges when a very poorly-dressed man approached her, whom she thought to be a beggar. She drew a coin from her pocket and offered it to him, but he politely refused it, and explained that he was not asking for money. Then he started to speak about God, very reverently but very ardently. Madame Guyon listened with surprise, her heart responding to all that he said, and when he went on to enlarge on the Holy Trinity it was as though she were hearing it for the first time. He spoke of the Mass, and of the care that should be taken by any who take part in it. Again she found herself agreeing with all that he said.

At last he spoke more personally. She had never met him before, and as her face was veiled he could not have known who she was, yet what he said revealed an intimate knowledge of her.

'I know, Madame, that you love God, that you are very charitable and give many alms to the poor,' he said, and went on to enumerate other virtues which had been developed in her. But then he went on, 'Yet you are very much astray. God desires something else from you.' He paused for a moment, then said clearly, 'You love your beauty.'

She walked silently on beside him, listening attentively to what he said, acquiescing with what he said about other faults of which she was aware, although it was the reference to her pride of appearance that impressed her most deeply. In later years she recalled his words about not merely being content to avoid the pains of hell, but arriving at such a state of perfection in this life that she would even avoid the pains of purgatory.[1] It was not so much fear of the pains of either hell or purgatory that worried her, however, but fear of grieving God. At that time in Paris, and later in Touraine where she also accompanied her husband, the consciousness of her attractive self was at once her source of natural pride and spiritual shame. And the two were in violent conflict.

'On this journey my vanity triumphed . . . I received many visits and much applause. My God, how clearly I see the folly of men, who let themselves be caught by a vain beauty! I hated passion,' she added. She admitted this more than once, and her husband easily detected it, petulantly telling her that since she loved God she had ceased from loving him. But although with him she had to fulfil her conjugal duty, she was under no such obligation to anyone else, and could enjoy seeing desire light up in amorous males who were stirred by her feminine charms. 'I hated passion . . . but I could not hate that in me which called it to life.' That in her which aroused a man's desire fed her pride, her self-love. She was ashamed of it, but try as she would she could not overcome it.

This particular form of vanity lay dormant when there was nothing, or no one, to stimulate it. She longed to go into a convent, where she would be completely shielded from all temptations to indulge that peacock-like propensity to display her charms. She talked it over with Mother Granger, Prioress of a Benedictine convent, who was the one person in whom she could confide, and to whom she went whenever she had the opportunity. As two of her sisters-in-law were nuns in the convent, it was easier for her to do so than would otherwise have been the case, although when her confessor and her mother-in-law realised the closeness of the friendship that had developed, they did everything in their power

[1] According to Roman Catholic theology eternal punishment and the guilt of mortal sin is absolved by the sacrament of penance, but if appropriate satisfaction has not been made for sins committed and absolved in life, satisfaction must be made after death, in purgatory, where the duration of time is limited, not in hell, where it is eternal.

to put an end to it. She discovered that Mother Granger too had had her problems with the Guyon family.

'I've been trying to please them for twenty years,' she said with a wry smile when Madame Guyon told of her vain attempts to win her mother-in-law's approval. 'Trying for twenty years without succeeding! So how can you expect to succeed in less than half that time!' Then she went on to give what advice she could. 'Give yourself up to God. Offer yourself to Him. Then, if He gives you this cross, carry it for love of Him,' was the gist of what she said. But in the case of the fight against natural vanity, all she could do was to give advice that was practical. Looking at the fashionably-dressed, beautiful woman in her full billowing skirts, her tight bodice and low-necked blouse, she remarked:

'I know your husband wishes you to be well-dressed, so you must follow the fashion – but is it necessary to expose so much of your neck and bosom? Wear a kerchief round your neck to cover it up. That will be much more modest and will attract less attention.' It was a simple enough thing to do, and did not deal with the basic problem, but at any rate it was a step in the right direction. Madame Guyon always wore a kerchief over a low-necked garment after that. Nor was it the only matter in which she followed the advice given by her mentor. Mother Granger was an unusually spiritually-minded woman for her day, completely loyal to the Roman Catholic church to which she had belonged all her life, with a suitable veneration for the saints who had worn hair shirts next to their skin, and in other ways demonstrated their devotion by inflicting pain upon themselves. All the same, her feet were on the ground. When she learned of the physical sufferings to which her young friend subjected herself, she wisely advised her to desist from doing anything that was harmful to her health. Her advice on all matters was followed implicitly, both the simple practical suggestions regarding the outer life, as well as the deeper inner lessons to be learned in trusting oneself totally to the will of God, come what may.

At that period of her life, the Benedictine Prioress was the closest friend Madame Guyon had, the one who more than any other encouraged her in the pilgrimage of her soul. But even the godly Prioress could not point the way to the deliverance from vanity that she longed for.

'I lamented my weakness. I made verses to express my trouble, but they served only to augment it. I prayed You, O my God, to take away this beauty, which had been so disastrous to me. I desired to lose it, or cease to love it.'

She felt as though she were being dragged in opposite directions. 'I was as if torn asunder, for on the outside my vanity dragged me, and within, the divine love. . . . As soon as I had the opportunity of exhibiting my vanity, I did it. And as soon as I had done it, I returned to you.' She could not lose her vanity, nor could she cease to love it. In her desperation she almost challenged God, 'Are You not strong enough to stop this?'

It was a cry from the heart, and the answer came quite soon, but in a form from which she would have shrunk if she had been told of it beforehand.

On arrival home from Touraine she was greeted with the news that her youngest child, a little girl, was down with smallpox. Intuitively Madame Guyon knew that she would be stricken with it, too. And so it happened. Her mother-in-law's stubbornness in refusing her the medical aid she needed nearly cost her life, but the providential appearance of a doctor who insisted on treating her saved it – but nothing could save her beauty. When the weeks of illness were drawing to a close and she was sufficiently restored to wonder what she looked like, the mirror revealed that her prayer 'take away this beauty' had been granted. The eyes that gazed back at her were the same, but the lids were inflamed and swollen. The contours of the cheekbones, the straight nose, the well-shaped mouth and chin had not changed, but the skin that covered them was like discoloured parchment, lifeless and pitted with pockmarks. Gone for ever was the fair, transparent complexion with its soft colourings, the faint blue shadings under the eyes, the rosy lips, the pink cheeks, the white forehead. Never again would men's eyes rest admiringly on her face – and never again would envious women whisper together that she was very skilful in applying make-up.

And never again would that peacock-like vanity that had drawn her attention away from God to herself have the power to do so.

It is impossible to delve the depths of that twenty-two-year-old girl's emotions as she faced the end of an era in her life. She would not have been human if she had not regarded that strangely unfamiliar-looking face with dismay, or have wondered what would be the reaction of others when they saw her. But beyond all that was the determined acceptance of what had happened as being the means of her deliverance. She would even further the work of destruction! She did nothing to alleviate the condition of her skin. She did not even try to protect it from further depredations. She refused to apply the herbal remedies that others had found effective, and went out of doors in all weathers even in bitingly cold winds which aggravated the pockmarks and inflamed them.

> 'To my God a heart of flame . . .
> To myself a heart of steel.'

'To myself a heart of steel.' It summed up her attitude, and the heart of steel refused to be moved by the piteous cries of despoiled nature. Madame Guyon's beauty, the cause of her vanity, had gone, and she would not bemoan it. Indeed, she could not bemoan it, for the contentment within her soul was deeper than it had ever been before. As she herself expressed it, 'The devastation without was counterbalanced by the peace within.'

Even the death of her second child, a little boy whom she loved dearly, could not disturb it, for although the blow overwhelmed her in one way, she found herself saying, as Job had said thousands of years before, 'The Lord gave. The Lord has taken away. Blessed be the name of the Lord.' And in some mystical way which she did not fully understand, came the assurance that a spiritual son would be given her in his place.

About eight months later she first met Francis La Combe, with whom her life was to be so strangely, even fatally, entwined.

A Benedictine nun, who is a most holy woman, in their refectory saw our Lord on the cross and the Holy Virgin near Him, and they appeared in great pain. They made movements which seemed to mark their sufferings and the desire they had to find someone who would be willing to share them. She ran to inform the Prioress. She said she was busy and could not go. In fact, she was amusing herself with flowers and trees. Not finding anyone who was willing to go, in great trouble she met and told me. I at once ran there, and our Lord appeared very pleased. He received and embraced me as if to associate me in His sufferings. . . .

Jeanne de la Mothe Guyon, while still in Montargis

4

Dark Night Ended

Francis La Combe was born in Thonon in Savoy, on the banks of Lake Geneva. He was a religious little boy, and early in life joined the Order of the Barnabites, with whom his natural talents were developed by a good education. By the year 1671 he was a tall, well-set man in his early twenties, and his first meeting with Madame Guyon was as the result of a letter he carried to her from her half-brother, Father de la Mothe.

Madame Guyon stood in some awe of Father de la Mothe, and not without reason. In the first place, his relationship as an elder brother put him in a position demanding her respect. Secondly, he was an ordained priest of the Church, and therefore to be venerated by all good Catholics. Thirdly, as later events were to prove, he was a clever and unscrupulous man whom it was wiser not to cross. So when she received a letter from him, urging her to receive the bearer of it and treat him as one of his most intimate friends, she had no option but to comply, although at the time she was in no mood to make fresh acquaintances.

Francis La Combe was therefore invited to the Guyon home, and there he met a pockmarked woman, some years his senior, simply dressed, graceful, courteous, and with whom he felt unusually free to talk about spiritual matters. This was surprising since she was a woman in the everyday world, married and with children, and not even a nun from the cloisters. But he had heard that two or three other Barnabites had been influenced by her, to the vast improvement of their spiritual lives, and had wondered why. Now, on meeting her, he began to understand.

'I have never seen a woman like this before,' he thought.

51

She seemed to be the possessor of an inner life which he could not define, and even as he talked to her husband, he was conscious of her. Yet not so much of her, as of an awareness of the presence of God. There was a quality of tranquillity in her silence which made him long to know its source. He therefore decided to call on the Guyons again, in the hope of having an opportunity to talk to her. That opportunity came quite inadvertently, for while he was chatting with her husband he suddenly felt faint and, excusing himself, went out into the garden to recover.

'Go and see if he's all right,' said Monsieur Guyon, crippled with gout, to his wife, and obediently she went. This was the very opportunity La Combe had desired. There was only a short time to talk, but it was sufficient for him to enquire and for her to explain the reality of what she called 'the inward way'.

God comes to dwell in the heart. He makes it His kingdom, bringing everything under His control. Jesus Christ had said, 'If a man loves me, he will keep my words and my Father will love him, and we will come unto him and make our abode with him.' It is there that He communes with us, speaks to us, reveals Himself. It is there, too, that the ego, the SELF, has to be dethroned, put to death.

She had little enough time for explanation, but little time is enough for divine revelation. Just as the Franciscan monk's two sentences to her had answered in a flash her questionings of years, so that conversation now answered La Combe's. He went away, as he said afterwards, changed into another man. God, the source of all spiritual power, was dwelling within him, and he returned to his native Savoy outwardly the same, but inwardly with a peace he had never known before. As for Madame Guyon,

'I preserved a root of esteem for him, for it appeared to me he would be God's. But I was very far from foreseeing that I should ever go to the place where he would be.'

They were not to meet again for nine years.

For him, those years were outwardly uneventful. A sincere

and earnest man who had early taken the vows of celibacy, he devoted himself to the religious life, developing into an unusually eloquent preacher, with administrative ability into the bargain.

He knew what was going on in the ecclesiastical world – the rise of the forthright Bossuet to a place of eminence at court, with his appointment as tutor to the Dauphin; of the problems connected with the status of the King's illegitimate children; of the tensions beginning to rise between the King and the Pope as to how far the divine right of each entitled them to supremacy in matters of earthly policy; and of the suspicion with which the King was viewing the increasing power of the Protestant nations, and, as a result, his changing attitude towards the Huguenots in his own realm. La Combe himself was by no means favourable to the Protestant faith, and viewed with disapproval its established position in Geneva. The movement towards reformation within Roman Catholicism itself was a different matter, in his view, and the emergence of Port Royalists, the Jansenites, the Quietists, commanded his respect if none of them claimed his allegiance. His deepest conscious desire was to please God, and he believed the way to do that was within the Order of the Barnabites, by adhering to their basic principles and practices, and cultivating his own inner life along the lines indicated in that illuminating interview with Madame Guyon.

For Madame Guyon herself, life was very different, and lived in a much less congenial atmosphere than that of a well-run monastery. The situation at home remained the same, with constant criticism and suspicious surveillance. Her happiest periods were when she was sufficiently ill to be left to herself. Then she could enter and enjoy the peace of that unseen world where, without interruption, she could listen to and speak to God. Even when, in July 1672, she suffered the double bereavement of her father and her little daughter, the inner peace balanced the natural grief, deeply as she felt it.

It was at this time that Mother Granger wrote to her, giving some instructions which she was expected to obey. She was to fast on St. Magdalene's Day, go to church wearing her signet ring, and on returning home go to her private closet, and there read a contract that had been prepared for her. This Madame Guyon did, and kneeling before an image of the child Jesus in the arms of his mother, she read the contract. It was very simple. It ran: 'I . . . promise to take for my spouse our Lord, the Child, and to give myself to Him for spouse, though unworthy.'

Kneeling there in the silence of her room with the contract before her, she made the deliberate, considered consecration of her life, her soul, her will, all that she was in herself, to Christ.

In one way it merely involved the ratification of the decision she had already made. Ever since the never-to-be-forgotten experience of realising the indwelling of God within her, her only ambition had been to belong unreservedly to Him. By putting her signature to that contract she was committing herself as irrevocably to Christ as the husband of her soul as when she signed the marriage contract which made Monsieur Guyon the husband of her body. And with her deep awareness of suffering as being the symbol of the Man, Christ Jesus, she prayed, not for blessing, not for fruitfulness, far less for spiritual gifts – and as for earthly prosperity, such a desire seems not to have entered her head. No, what she prayed for was 'crosses, scorn, confusion, disgrace and ignominy', and the grace to bear them all with the meekness of Christ.

She sealed the contract with her ring, on July 22nd, 1672.

It was to her a sacred festival, alone there in her room. 'O Divine Spouse, it seems to me that you then made of me your living temple, and that you yourself consecrated it as churches are consecrated.' With her colourful imagination she applied the signs used in the consecration of churches to herself. 'As churches are marked with the sign of the cross, you marked me also with the same sign. . . . And as at the consecration of churches there are candles, which are lighted in the place for the crosses, and the candle represents faith and charity, so I have ground to believe that you have not permitted those virtues to abandon me since that time. But as the characteristic of the candle is to gradually consume itself by its own fire, and to destroy itself by the light and heat which make it live, so it seemed to me that it was necessary for my heart to be perfectly destroyed by this fire of love.'

This experience, while deepening her inner sense of security, also made her much more sensitive. There were times when the awareness of God's presence was withdrawn, and she usually found that the reason for it was self-pity, or a subconscious rebellion against circumstances, or even a secret complacency in her own faithfulness. Self dies hard. It has so many subtle forms of apparent virtue that when one appears to have been dealt with, another rears its head. She hated them all as they were revealed to her in their true light. The Spirit of God was working deeper and deeper within her, and with the decreasing satisfaction in her own virtues there came, unknown to herself, an increasing evidence of His presence in her. Others noticed it. 'I have seen your niece,' said a worldly-minded man to an aunt of her husband's, and added, 'One can see she never loses the presence of God.' She was very surprised when this remark was reported to her, not only that she should have been the subject of it, but also because, 'I did not think he understood what it was to have God present in this way.' She was surprised, too, when the wife of the governor of the town, whom she met from time to time socially, came to her one day and said, 'God drew me so powerfully yesterday that I cannot hold out against Him. I've come to tell you so.'

They had been together when another woman had entered into conversation and spoken in a very learned way about spiritual things, having studied the Fathers and arrived at certain conclusions about God which she aired authoritatively. She had spoken with finality, evidently feeling there was nothing more to be said. She had spoken with such assurance that Madame Guyon was repelled, but had remained quiet, feeling grieved at hearing God discussed in such a way. But evidently what the woman had said had impressed the governor's wife? In some way, God Himself had drawn her through that conversation. So she assumed, but she was wrong.

'Oh, it wasn't what *she* said,' explained the governor's wife quickly. 'It wasn't her talking – it was your silence. It was your silence that spoke to me, in the depths of my heart. I could not enjoy what she was saying to me at all.'

Her silence. There had been a greater eloquence in it than in the flood of words gushing from the woman who seemed to know everything, and she knew whose voice had reached the heart of her friend. It was the voice of her divine Bridegroom. 'I stand at the door and knock. If any man hear my voice and open the door, I will come in. . . .' All that was needed was to explain to her that God had come to make His kingdom within her, and all she had to do was to let Him in. The transformation in the life and character of the governor's wife was lasting after that – as for Madame Guyon, she began to realise how her own death to self was resulting in life to others.

*   *   *

Monsieur Guyon was often ill, and he began to be very worried as to what would happen to all his great wealth when he died. 'As he had no children but my eldest son, who was often at the gates of death, he wished extremely to have heirs.' He therefore made a special journey to obtain the intercession of St. Edme on his behalf, and 'he was heard, and God gave me another son'.

Those months were the happiest she had yet experienced. She knew such uninterrupted peace and joy of heart that it was like entering a new life. Even the suffering of the difficult confinement was more than compensated for by the fact that she was so ill she had to be kept quiet and undisturbed, free from all distractions. The solitude was a relief. 'I endeavoured to compensate myself for the little leisure I had at other seasons for praying, and remaining alone with God.' As for the pain and the weakness, was this not just what she had prayed for? Her ardent soul would not have been fully satisfied without it.

But this halcyon period was not to last. It proved to be the preparation for the darkest years of her life, years in which all the delicious feelings that had supported her inwardly subsided, dissolved, vanished altogether, leaving her bewildered like a child in the dark, who has suddenly been forsaken.

It started with the death of the woman who had been to her a spiritual mother – Mother Granger, the Prioress. When she heard of it, she was overwhelmed. The one person who really understood her, the one person to whom she knew she could safely reveal all that was in her mind, had gone. 'I declare that this blow was the most severely felt of any I yet had.' What made the blow the more acute was that it was totally unexpected, and that she had had no intimation of her friend's condition. This distressed her. That invisible bond between them had been so strong that on several occasions they had been aware of each other's thoughts and feelings, even though separated by long distances, and without opportunity for verbal communication. When her own father was taken ill she had known of it intuitively before the news reached her. Why then had she been left without that mystical enlightenment that Mother Granger, who was spiritually closer to her than anyone else, was dying? Had she but known, she might have had the opportunity to go and see her, to receive some last loving message or exhortation that would support her in her loss and give her direction for the future. But as it was, 'I felt myself utterly deserted, inwardly and outwardly. I thought only of the loss I sustained in a person who would have conducted me on a road where I no longer found track nor path.'

That trackless way was already spreading out before her,

for she realised that her reaction to the death of Mother
Granger was quite different to that when her father and her
little daughter had died within days of each other. Her grief
then had been balanced by an inexplicable inward peace.
Now there was no such comfort. There was only a deadness.
It was as though God had withdrawn himself. And as time
went on, she was dismayed to find how different she herself
was from what she had been. She seemed to be disinclined for
all she had formerly longed for. That fervent love for God was
there no more. She felt there must be something terribly
wrong with her, and in order to rectify this state of affairs she
reverted to some of her former practices. 'I used all sorts of
penances, prayers, pilgrimages, vows.' But they were useless. The heavens seemed like brass. She had long since
ceased praying to the saints, but now she would have
besought the Virgin Mary to intercede on her behalf if she
could have believed she would hear her.

'The Holy Virgin, for whom I had had a very great and
tender devotion from my youth, appeared to me inaccessible.
I did not know whom to turn to for help, either in heaven or
earth. If I tried to find God in my heart, to find Him who once
had possessed it so powerfully, not only did I find nothing
there, but I was even repelled with violence.' Her own heart
condemned her. She was the worst of sinners.

The time was to come when she would write, '. . . I saw
there was no salvation for me in myself . . . I was, O divine
Jesus, that lost sheep of the house of Israel that You were
come to save. You were truly the Saviour of her who could
find no salvation out of You,' and then add recklessly, 'O
men, strong and holy, find salvation as much as you please in
what you have done, that is holy and glorious for God; as for
me, I make my boast only in my weaknesses, since they have
earned for me such a Saviour!'

But that time had not come yet, and years were to pass
before she could assert it with such freedom. Now she was
only conscious of feeling devoid of God's presence, of being
without those ecstatic feelings that had buoyed her up, and of

being oppressed by the sense of her own intrinsic sinfulness, which had soiled even the good she had tried to do.

Gone were the periods of ecstatic joy when it seemed she was transported to realms far beyond human telling. Gone was the ineffable sense of God's presence, stirring her to love and adoration, quickening her desire to please Him, sacrifice for Him, suffer for Him. The spiritual darkness into which she found herself slipping left her without any urge either to worship God or befriend man. She was only oppressed by the sense of her own sinfulness. Yet the sinfulness of which she was aware was not that against which she had battled earlier. The faults of vanity, the propensity for lying, the secrets of lusts – these had been dealt with through genuine confession and sincere repentance. What oppressed her now was the sense of her inbuilt sinfulness which had soiled even the good she had tried to do.

Even her apparently righteous acts now appeared filthy. 'All appeared to me full of defects; my charities, my alms, my prayers, my penances, all rose up against me as objects of condemnation. My conscience was a witness I could not appease, and yet strangely, it was not the sin of my youth that caused my pain. It was not they that bore witness against me; it was a universal witness that in all the good I had done there were sentiments of evil.' The inexplicable thing was that she could not put her finger on any specific sins or faults. 'As a consequence I did not find any remedy for my ills in confession.' What a relief it would have been to have enumerated her iniquities and shortcomings in the confessional box! Any penances imposed would have been welcomed, however harsh. But she knew that if she tried to explain her guilt to her confessor he would have commended her on her humility. He would not have understood.

No one, it seemed, could understand her state. There was no one to tell her that others had passed that way, experiencing what some of the mystics referred to as 'the dark night of the soul'. Even the Franciscan monk, who had first spoken to her of God making His kingdom in her heart,

gave her no help now. The flood of words that poured from
her pen was as bewildering to him as her own state was to
her, and she did not express herself clearly. Eventually he
told her to stop writing to him – he had had enough of it.
Likewise the Jesuit Father, formerly very sympathetic
towards her. Another cleric, a Jansenist, offended that she
did not respond to his special line of teaching, openly
preached about her, saying that she who had once been an
example to all the town through her good works, was now a
scandal. Certainly, the urge to help the poor had left her, and
if she forced herself to go and see them, she had nothing to
say. She seemed powerless to do anything for anybody.
Before the birth of her fifth child, a girl, she gave way to such
paroxysms of sobbing when alone that she marvelled there
was not a miscarriage. It was as though she was deranged at
times. If she had lived in the twentieth century she would
probably have been sent to a psychiatric hospital. As it was,
she felt forsaken by God and man, for everybody seemed to
disapprove of her, and when by chance anyone praised her, she
blushed with shame – they did not know what a hypocrite she
was! 'If I endeavoured to exhibit an outward righteousness
by the practice of some good, my heart secretly gave the lie to
my action; I saw it was hypocrisy to appear what I was not.'

   Although she remained in this state, on and off, for seven
years, there were occasions when a certain practical ability
was made evident that surprised everyone, herself more than
all. One had to do with no less a person than Monsieur, the
King's brother. One of the most notorious characters in
French history, Monsieur was often in need of money, and
had no scruples as to how he obtained it. It was not difficult,
therefore, for someone to concoct a story, in his name, to the
effect that Madame Guyon and her brother owed him two
hundred thousand livres. Her husband angrily washing his
hands of the whole affair, she had no one to whom to turn for
help, and it was not until the very day when the case was to
be decided that, after Mass, she felt strongly urged to go to
see the judges herself. So to the judges she went.

'I was extremely surprised to find that I knew all the twists and turns of this business, without knowing how I had been able to learn it. The first judge was so surprised to see a thing so different from what he thought, that he himself urged me to go and see the other judges.' The upshot of that affair was that, since the face of Monsieur had to be saved, judgment was given in his favour – but to the tune of one hundred and fifty livres, instead of two hundred thousand demanded.

It was one of the few occasions when Madame Guyon's husband expressed himself very pleased at what she had done. He had no cause for complaint, either, when at the instigation of his mother, he demanded that she should give account of the money entrusted to her for housekeeping. It was suggested that she gave so much to charity, she was almost certainly running into debt. Once again, she acquitted herself well.

'I did not write any of my alms, and my expense was found right without a franc more or less. I was amazed, and saw that my charities were given out of God's capital.' She learned through that experience what many of God's servants have learned down through the ages – that He is no man's debtor. 'Oh, if people only knew how charities, far from inconveniencing, bring plenty!' she wrote. 'What useless extravagance there is which might maintain the poor, and which God would repay. . . .'

Not long after that incident her husband was taken seriously ill, and eventually died, but not before his attitude towards her had changed completely. As she knelt beside his bed one day, and asked his forgiveness for any way in which she had displeased him, he was evidently deeply moved, and said, 'It is I who ask your pardon. I did not deserve you.'

From that time on, knowing he was dying, he showed he was glad to have her with him, and gave her advice as to what she should do after his death. He died on the eve of St. Magdalene's Day. It was a significant date for her.

Exactly four years had passed since she had signed the contract Mother Granger had given her, in which she

consecrated herself to Christ. Now she was free, and had it
not been for her children, she would have entered a convent
and become a nun. This is what she would have desired, but
as it was, instead of the peace of a convent, she found herself
plunged into business affairs for which she had little
preparation, and no experience. Her husband's affairs were
in rather a chaotic condition and it took her days to sort them
out. Then, among his securities, she found papers belonging
to other people. These had evidently been deposited with
him for safe keeping and must now be returned.

'I made an exact inventory for each person with my own
hand, and sent them to those to whom they belonged. This
would have been very difficult for me, O my God, without
Your help, because, owing to the long time my husband had
been ill, everything was in great disorder. This got me the
reputation of a clever woman,' she commented naively, 'as
well as another affair which happened.' And she went on to
relate it.

'A great number of persons, who were mutually litigating
for more than twenty years, applied to my husband to
reconcile them. Although it was not the business of a
gentleman, they entreated him because he had uprightness
and a good intellect; so, as there were among those persons
some he loved, he consented to it.

'There were twenty suits, one against the other, and there
were twenty-two people who were litigating in this way,
without any one being able to end their difference, owing to
new incidents that arose every day. My husband undertook
to engage advocates to examine their papers, but he died
without having done anything. After his death I sent to fetch
them to give back their papers, but they would not receive
them, and begged me to reconcile them and prevent their
ruin. It appeared to me alike ridiculous and impossible that I
should undertake so serious a business, and one so long in
dispute. Yet, supported by Your strength, O my God, I
followed the movement you gave me to consent. I shut myself
up for more than thirty days in my closet on this business,

without leaving it save for Mass and meals. These worthy people all blindly signed their compromise without seeing it. They were so pleased about it they could not help publishing it everywhere.'

Little wonder that young Madame Guyon, not yet thirty, was becoming a well-known personality in Montargis. Little wonder, too, that those who were her friends, some in influential positions, urged her, now that her husband was dead, to separate from her mother-in-law. The older woman's bad temper, and rudeness to her daughter-in-law, was well known.

'I answered them I had no ground's to complain of her, and that I counted on remaining with her if she would allow me. It was the view You from the first gave me, O my God, not to descend from the cross, as You yourself had not descended from it. For this reason I resolved not only not to leave my mother-in-law, but even not to get rid of the maid of whom I have spoken.'

And so, for the next three years, she remained in the house with her mother-in-law until at last, following a visit she made on business to a neighbouring town, things came to a head.

It so happened that in that particular town there lived some relatives of her mother-in-law, who had always treated her with warmth and courtesy, vying with each other to entertain her. Now, to her astonishment, their attitude had changed completely. So far from being cordial, they were quite antagonistic, and then it was that she heard that her mother-in-law had complained to them about her, telling them how unkind she was to her, and how unhappy she made her.

Poor Madame Guyon! She had always thought of herself as being the one who was ill-used, and undoubtedly she was, but it had never occurred to her that her mother-in-law might be feeling the same. It is given to few, if any of us, to know the effect we have on other people, 'to see ourselves as others see us.' It had never crossed her mind that to an outspoken woman like her mother-in-law her docility might have been taken for contempt, her well-meant efforts to please for derision, and that the very suppression of her natural instincts almost certainly created an indefinable atmosphere of pent-up forces which might erupt violently at any time. On her own showing she behaved very strangely at times, with eyes wide open looking around in church when everyone else was reverently bowed, retreating silently into herself in company, seeking spiritual help from well-known ecclesiastics then withdrawing when they offered it. As she herself admitted many years later, she may have unwittingly irritated her mother-in-law beyond what a quick-tempered woman could endure. 'She had a very good heart, but her temper was perhaps there in spite of her . . . She had virtue and intelligence, and putting aside certain failings, which people who do not use prayer keep ignorant of, she had good qualities.'

However, she saw nothing else but her own pitiable situation at the time, and when she got home, determined to have the matter out.

'People are saying I make you unhappy,' she said. 'I am sorry. I have tried to please you, I really have. You know I don't like this house. I've only stayed because I thought you wanted me to. But I've no intention of living with you if it only gives you trouble. I'll leave, and go somewhere else rather than make things difficult for you.'

'Do what you like,' said her mother-in-law coldly. 'I haven't spoken of it to anyone, but I've made up my mind to keep house separately now.'

So that was that. 'This was fairly giving me my dismissal.' The relief of feeling free at last to move away was tempered by the consciousness that it was the dead of winter, and she had nowhere to go. 'I did not know what to do. I saw myself obliged to turn out in the depth of winter with the children and their nurse, without knowing what would become of us.' But she was a very wealthy woman, and although there was no suitable house in the town for her then, the Benedictines provided her with an apartment until she found a place in the country – and then the tide began to turn.

* * *

It was during this long unhappy period of spiritual darkness that one of her footmen came to tell her that he wanted to become a Barnabite. She wrote to her brother, Father de la Mothe, about it, and he told her she should get in touch with Father La Combe, who was now Superior of the Barnabites in Thonon.

Father La Combe! That young Barnabite who had shown such a desire for the same personal relationship with God as she had been enjoying at the time when they met, years ago! So now he had advanced so far in his Order as to be a Superior, while she was so debased that she doubted whether there was any hope for her. She seemed to be past caring whether she did wrong or not. 'I found myself hard towards God, insensible to his bounties. There was not shown me any good that I had done in all my life. The good appeared to me evil, and what is frightful is that this state appeared to me bound to endure eternally . . .' That was her inward condition when her footman's request and her brother's instruction made it necessary for her to write to Father La Combe.

'I was very glad of this opportunity of asking him to pray for me. I wrote to him that I had fallen from the grace of God, that I had repaid God's benefits by the blackest ingratitude; in short, that I was abjectness itself, and a subject deserving compassion; and that, far from having advanced towards my God, I had entirely alienated myself from Him.'

She was slightly eased after writing that letter. It had alleviated the strain to expose her innermost thoughts to someone who she felt might understand, although, about the same time, she was horrified to find that the city of Geneva came repeatedly to her mind. Geneva! Hotbed of the Calvinistic heresy! It would be the end of all hope if she drifted so far as to quit the true faith for apostasy!

Then came a reply from Father La Combe. It was infinitely reassuring. Far from rebuking or condemning her, as had others, he assured her that she had *not* fallen from grace. The fact that she was so stricken with the consciousness of her sinfulness was evidence of that. He went on to tell her something of his own spiritual experiences, some of which were very similar to her own. The effect of this letter was to bring peace of mind, and a calming of spirit, and a renewal of hope that perhaps, after all, she was not damned. A dream she had was strangely comforting, too, as it seemed to contain a message from God. She saw a little nun with a beatific expression, who came to her and said, 'My sister, I come to tell you that God wishes you at Geneva.' That set her mind at rest. If God sent a message to tell her He wanted her there, He must have a purpose in it, though she did not know what it could be.

It was the month of July, and St. Magdalene's Day was approaching. Every year, in spite of her spiritual depression, she had commemorated her contract of spiritual marriage on that day, and the thought came to her that she would like Father La Combe to say the Mass for her on that day. So she wrote to him and asked him to do so, although she doubted whether the letter would reach him in time.

The day dawned – St. Magdalene's Day, 1680. It was a day she would never forget, imprinted indelibly in her memory. 'It was this happy day of the Magdalene that my soul was perfectly delivered from all her troubles,' she wrote, although how and where it happened her diary did not divulge. The dark cloud of depression was lifted completely, all the peace and joy and love she had known before returned, but with a difference. 'My trouble and my pain were changed into a peace such that, the better to explain, I call God-peace. The peace I possessed before this time was indeed the peace of God – peace, the gift of God – but it was not God-peace; peace which He possesses in Himself, and which is found only in Him.'

She was not able to express clearly the joy that was now

hers. 'One day of this happiness would be indeed the recompense with usury for many years of suffering. O Paul! You say that the sufferings of this life are not worthy to be compared with the glory that is prepared for us!' she continued ecstatically. 'It is true even in this life, I can say from actual experience.' She felt it was too good to last, but as time went on she found that the inner stability and liberty and peace increased rather than diminished, and that all her former conscious love for God and desire to help others, especially the poor, had returned.

She had changed outwardly, too. She was still the same person, yet there was a simple, unaffected spontaneity about her which had been lacking before. The self-consciousness which had revealed itself in a variety of ways, sometimes an awkward reserve, sometimes an excess of zeal or piety, that had robbed her personality of simplicity, had gone. She was perfectly natural in her behaviour, going about the ordinary affairs of life cheerfully and without affectation. Yet, with her analytical mind, she realised that something had happened that she could not altogether account for.

'That intellect which I once thought I had lost in a strange stupidity, was restored to me with additions. I was astonished at it myself, and I found that there was nothing for which it was not able, and in which it did not succeed. Those who saw me said I had a prodigious intellect. I know well that I had but little intellect, but that in God my mind had taken a quality which before it was without. It experienced, it seemed to me, something of the state in which the apostles were after having received the Holy Spirit.'

She heard from Father La Combe soon afterwards. Yes, her letter had arrived in time, and to his surprise, as he was bringing her before God during the Mass, an inner voice had said to him three times, 'You shall both dwell in the same place.' Furthermore, God had told him He had great designs for her. That was all he knew but he passed on to her what he had been told.

She did not pay too much attention to it at the time. It seemed very unlikely that God had anything special for her to do, a pockmarked widow with three children, and with only a sketchy sort of education obtained in convents in a provincial town. But there were some things she could do, and she set about doing them with vigour, renewing her charitable acts to the poor, setting some of them up in business, and especially ensuring that pretty girls were taught a skill that would provide them with an honest livelihood. She knew the temptations that would otherwise assail them. She tended a number of sick people, too, with such success that she gained a reputation for healing those whom the surgeon had given up as incurable.

She was free now as she had never been before, free to worship as well as to work. 'What happiness did I not taste in my little solitude and my little household, where nothing interrupted my repose! My young children did not require too much of my attention, as they were in good hands, so I went into the woods where I spent as many happy days as I had spent months of grief.'

She could happily have spent the rest of her life in that place, bringing up her children, doing all the good possible in the neighbourhood, attending church and retreats and festivals to her heart's content. Everything was turning out well. Amazingly, even her mother-in-law's attitude towards her changed. What brought this about it would be difficult to say, but it was partly, at any rate, a discovery the old woman made concerning her daughter-in-law's opportunities for re-marriage. Three men in high social positions had proposed marriage, and she had refused them all, but had said nothing about it to anyone. Old Madame Guyon had sometimes taunted her about her lack of suitors, telling her friends that her daughter-in-law hadn't re-married because she had never had the chance. When she learned from other sources what the true situation was, she was rather abashed, and although she never apologised, she began to speak so highly of her daughter-in-law, and to show her such affection, that Madame Guyon observed of that period that she had no crosses to bear at all.

Nevertheless, she was careful not to settle down into this congenial form of existence, as though it would continue indefinitely. 'I kept myself in expectancy, with a firm will to execute God's orders at the expense of my own life when He should make them known.' All the same, when the intimation came, it was unexpected, and took her by surprise.

She had gone to Paris on business, and, as was her custom, entered a church to make her confession. She went to the first confessor to be found, made her confession, which was a very short one, and was prepared to be dismissed when the man said to her, 'I don't know who you are. I don't know whether you are married or single, or a widow. But I feel very strongly that I should tell you that you must do what our Lord has made you know He desires of you. That is all I have to say.'

'But Father, I am a widow,' she answered. 'I have three children, two of them under six. What else could God desire of me, but to bring them up?'

'I know nothing about that,' was the answer. 'You know whether God has made you recognise that He wishes something of you. If it is so, there is nothing that should hinder you from doing His will. One must even leave one's children to do it.'

She made no answer, and went away, but in her heart, she knew what it meant. Geneva. She should go to Geneva.

Just about that time a Dominican monk who was a friend of hers came to visit her, and she talked it over with him. He told her he would pray about it for three days, and then give her his opinion. At the end of the three days he told her he believed it was God's will she should go there, but in order to be sure, she ought to see the Bishop of Geneva. After all, she would be going into his diocese and it was only right that he should be consulted. He also advised her to write to Father La Combe, to ask for his prayers, since he was also living in that area.

It was at this point that she ran into difficulties. Father La Combe not only prayed about it himself, but invited some godly women of his acquaintance to do so too. They all agreed, unanimously, that she should go to Geneva. In addition, a Benedictine nun, a nun of the Visitation, and a Father Claude Martin all gave the same opinion, independently of each other. With so much evidence to confirm her own conviction, there seemed no reason to change her course – except for one thing.

The Bishop of Geneva did not agree with them.

He was not unsympathetic. Quite the reverse, in fact. He thoroughly approved of her resolve to come into his diocese, wealthy woman that she was, and with a reputation for piety and good works. The only thing in which he did not agree was the exact whereabouts of her calling. He did not think Geneva itself was the right place – she should go to Gex, where the New Catholics were starting a work. She should go and join them.

'But I have no call to Gex,' she remonstrated. 'God has called me to Geneva.'

'There is nothing to stop you visiting Geneva,' he replied. 'It is only a few miles from Gex. It is to Gex I think you should go.' So with her invariable habit of bowing to authority, she agreed to go to Gex – but not to join the New Catholics, as he urgently suggested. She could not deny her inner conviction to that extent. She would go to Gex, she would give all her money to the New Catholics for their work there, she would live with them, but she would not become one of them. The idea she had had of going quietly to the city of Geneva, getting a small apartment there, and commencing to do simple medical work, using her skills in that way to help people, and especially to strengthen the few Catholics who were there, had to be abandoned. She would go to Gex, as the Bishop insisted, and there she would commit her way to God, to show her what she should do. So she sold her home, left her two older children, boys, in the care of guardians ('although I was extremely grieved to leave my younger son, the confidence I had in the Holy Virgin, to whom I had vowed him, and whom I looked on as my mother, calmed all my griefs'), gave a huge sum of money to the New Catholics, and with her little daughter, a nun and two maids, set out for the unknown.

The Soul That Loves God
Finds Him Everywhere

Oh Thou, by long experience tried,
Near whom no grief can long abide;

My Love! How full of sweet content
I pass my years of banishment:

All scenes alike engaging prove
To souls impressed with sacred Love:
Where'er they dwell, they dwell in Thee;
In heaven, in earth, or on the sea.

To me remains no place nor time
My country is in every clime;
I can be calm and free from care
On any shore, since God is there.

While place we seek, or place we shun
The soul finds happiness in none;
But with a God to guide our way,
'Tis equal joy to go or stay.

Could I be cast where Thou art not,
That were indeed a dreadful lot;
But regions none remote I call,
Secure of finding God in all.

My country, Lord, art Thou alone;
No other can I claim or own;
The point where all my wishes meet;
My Law, my Love; life's only sweet:

I hold by nothing here below;
Appoint my journey, and I go . . .

Jeanne de la Mothe Guyon

5

Into the Unknown

When wealthy young widows, noted for piety and good works, suddenly steal away, apparently deserting their children, and make for some remote destination with the idea of serving God there, it is inevitable that people will talk. Madame Guyon had slipped off very quietly, rather fearful that attempts would be made to stop her, but when it was realised that she had placed her six-year-old son with her cousin, a counsellor of Parliament, whom she had made her children's guardian, and that she had given an enormous sum of money to the New Catholics, there was quite a furore among those who knew her. Opinions were sharply divided as to the rights and wrongs of what she had done. There were those who asserted that her duty was to stay in Montargis and bring up her children. There were others who were overcome with admiration at the sacrifice she was making and the dedication she showed. Some of these, like the Duchess of Charost, had friends at Court, where religion had taken a new turn, with one of the King's mistresses taking the veil, another departing in high dudgeon to her estate in the country, and the King himself, a reformed character, having only a platonic friendship with his children's demure and pious governess, Madame de Maintenon. A mild interest in the provincial heiress was being aroused in Paris.

All of which was intensely provoking to Father de la Mothe. After all, when one's young half-sister has been successfully married off to a very wealthy man, and then been left a widow, one expects to derive some personal benefit, and to have an authoritative voice in the disposal of her money. Instead of this, the self-willed creature had not only not given him the annuity he was expecting, but had donated what he had hoped would be coming his way to an organisation with which he was not even connected.

His reaction to the news he got about her boded no good for Madame Guyon who, by this time, was well on her way to Gex.

The journey there was punctuated with various dangers, through which she and her little party came without serious injury, and 'the external gaiety' she preserved reassured the fearful among them. As for her, she was so happy and carefree that she sang aloud, glad to be done, as she thought, with the entanglements of wealth and worldliness, feeling that, like the Israelites of old, she was being led by a pillar of cloud by day and a pillar of fire by night.

It was not that she expected things to be easy, or that she was left in ignorance that trials awaited her. Her own little girl was an unconscious prophet during that journey, her childish occupations containing a significance which Madame Guyon herself recognised.

'What was astonishing was that in the boat my daughter, without knowing what she was doing, could not help making crosses. She kept a person employed in cutting rushes, and then she made them into crosses and quite covered me with them. She put more than three hundred on me. I let her do it, and I understood inwardly that there was a mystery in what she was doing. There was given to me an inward certainty that I was going there only to reap crosses, and that this little girl was sowing the Cross for me to gather.

'Sister Garnier, who saw that whatever they did they could not prevent the child from loading me with crosses, said to me, "What this child is doing is very mysterious," then said to her, "My little lady, put crosses on me also." She answered, "They are not for you; they are for my dear mother." She gave Sister Garnier one to please her, then she continued putting them on me. When she had put on a very great number she had river-flowers given to her, which were found on the water, and making a wreath with them she placed it on my head and said to me, "After the

Cross you will be crowned." In silence I wondered at all this . . .'

And sailing along on the quiet waters she offered herself afresh to her Lord for whatever He might call upon her to suffer. He had suffered, and she wanted to enter into that fellowship with Him. It was a further step, taken deliberately, of conformity to His will.

About the same time a friend of hers, a nun, had a vision about her, which was related to her later. 'She saw my heart in the midst of a great number of thorns, so that it was quite covered with them, and said that our Lord appeared in this heart, very well pleased; and she saw that the more strongly the thorns pricked, instead of being disfigured my heart appeared more beautiful, and our Lord was more pleased.'

So she travelled on, and events were so timed that she arrived at Annecy on the even of St. Magdalene's Day. Annecy! It was always associated in her mind with St. Francis de Sales. She had reached the very place where was the tomb of the man whose life and writings had so inspired her, on the very day when she always renewed the vows she had made to Christ. It was a notable experience. The Bishop of Geneva met her there, and said a Mass for her, and the words 'I will espouse thee in faith, I will espouse thee for ever' were deeply impressed on her mind.

'I honoured the relics of St. Francis de Sales with whom our Lord gave me a particular union. I say union, for it appeared to me that the soul in God is united with the saints more or less as they are conformed to her, and then those saints are rendered more intimately present to her in God Himself.' To her these saints were friends, united by God in an immortal bond. Her spiritual friendships were not limited to those she had known in the flesh, like Mother Granger. 'The whole family, in heaven and on earth' contained those whose experiences she could relate to, whose examples and words had reached her heart. St. Francis de Sales, though he had died before she was born, was one of them. He, too, had been drawn to Geneva, he too believed that ordinary people like herself could know and love God. She felt she was in the right succession.

But she did not stay more than twenty-four hours in Annecy. The next stop was Geneva itself, and another Mass, at the house of the French Resident. 'I had much joy in communicating, and it seemed to me that God bound me there even more strongly to Himself.' But she did not stay there, either. That very day she travelled on to Gex, arriving at her destination late in the evening, and it was there that everything suddenly began to go wrong.

No preparation had been made for them. An empty apartment awaited them, just four bare walls. There was not even a bed, although the Bishop had assured her that it was furnished.

'Apparently he thought so. We slept at the Sisters of Charity, who had the kindness to give us their beds. . . .' But Madame Guyon could not sleep. 'I suffered a pain and agony which can be better experienced than described.' For she became aware that her little girl was not well. She had evidently not noticed it before, for the child had been very lively on the journey, but now she was weak and listless, and Madame Guyon was overwhelmed with self-accusation. Why had she brought the child to such a place, forcing her to share the privation she was quite prepared to endure herself? All confidence that she had done the right thing deserted her that night, and lying in her narrow bed she could not restrain her tears. The whole thing had been a mistake! She ought never to have left home. Suppose her little girl died! It would be her fault. 'I saw her as a victim whom I had sacrificed by my imprudence.' Then she rememberd that there was an Ursuline convent in Thonon, about twenty miles away. The child would be better off with the Ursulines, who specialised in training and caring for little girls. She would take her there the very next day!

But next day, when she explained her plan, she found herself unexpectedly opposed. She was not helped, but deliberately hindered, in making arrangements to go to

Thonon. She was in a strange neighbourhood where she knew no one, she had given away her money, and now was more or less at the mercy of the New Catholics to whom she had given it. They were determined to keep her within their own community. She was at her wits' end when suddenly she thought of the young Barnabite in whom she had always taken an interest since the time he visited her home years ago – Father La Combe. Father La Combe was in Thonon. She would write to him. This she did, begging him to come and see her and advise her, for she was terribly anxious about the health of her little girl. And as he had a letter from the Bishop of Geneva about the same time, urging him to go and see Madame Guyon who had just arrived from Paris and was rather upset, he went promptly.

It was in these circumstances that the two met again. Although their first and only personal conversation had taken place years before, as soon as they saw each other they were conscious of an affinity of spirit difficult to describe, but of which both were aware. 'There was in it nothing human or natural,' Madame Guyon wrote later. The very absence of personal attraction enabled them to speak freely, not only of their personal spiritual experiences, but of the immediate problem confronting her. To her relief he told her at once that she should take her little daughter to Thonon, where she would be well looked after by the Ursulines. Then she confided in him that she did not feel at all easy with the New Catholics, and that others had warned her not to join them.

'I don't believe God requires it of you, either,' he said. 'But I think you should remain with them, without committing yourself to anything, until God makes it plain, perhaps through circumstances, whether you should leave or stay.' So with Father La Combe as an escort she took her little girl to Thonon, and remained with her for a fortnight at the Ursulines. The child did not get on as well there as she expected, and Madame Guyon who, in spite of her own readiness to take the vows of poverty, chastity and obedience, had no intention of imposing them on her children, was dismayed to realise that the child's education would suffer there.

'With her natural disposition it seemed she would have done wonders if educated in France, and that I was depriving her of all this, and putting it out of her power to do anything, or to find in the future proposals of marriage such as she might hope for.' A good marriage to a man of rank was what it was her duty to provide for her daughter – what else was there in life for a young woman? But a girl brought up in Savoy, with a provincial accent and provincial manners, lacking finesse and social poise, would be at a disadvantage, as Madame Guyon very well knew.

'For thirteen days I suffered a trouble inconceivable. All that I had given up seemed to have cost me nothing in comparison with what the sacrifice of my daughter cost me.' But through it all she began to see there was a purpose of sanctification in her own soul. 'I believe, O my God, that You caused this to purify the too human attachment I had for her natural gifts.' There remained a streak of worldly pride, known to a later age as snobbishness, if not for herself at least for the child she loved, and it had to go. Not without a struggle did she reach the point of renunciation, and, leaving her child in Thonon, return to Gex. Incidentally, as soon as she left, the child's health began to improve.

The fortnight in Thonon had been fraught with some traumatic experiences, one at least of which was connected with Father La Combe. She met a hermit living in the neighbourhood, a man renowned in the vicinity for his holiness, whose life-style resembled that of John the Baptist. He told her that God had revealed to him that He had great designs for her and for Father La Combe, that their destiny was to help souls – but that strange trials awaited them both. He did not try to minimise their intensity, though he did not know what they would be. As far as she was concerned, an unexpected one awaited her on her return to Gex.

A letter awaited her from her half-brother, Father de la Mothe, and as she read it she realised he had not been idle.

All the best people, he told her, the pious, the professionals, the gentlemen, were united in condemning her for the course she was taking. Furthermore, her mother-in-law had been so shocked by her departure that she had suddenly become senile, and therefore the children's inheritance was in jeopardy. (This turned out to be quite untrue, but she had no reason to doubt it at the time.) See what she had brought upon her family! His was not the only letter that reached her. Others came from various sources, some accusing her quite violently, and there were times when she felt submerged by it all. Yet somehow, there was a deeper peace of heart than she had known before. Perhaps it was this that enabled her not to show outwardly what she was suffering inwardly – for there was no doubt about her suffering.

'I shut myself up as much as I could, and there I allowed myself to be penetrated by the pain, which appeared to me very profound. I bore it very passively without being able, or even wishing, to alleviate it . . . It appeared to me that I then commenced to bear troubles in a divine manner, and from this time forward, without any sentiment, the soul could be at the same time very happy and very pained, afflicted and beatified.

'It was not in at all the same way I had borne my first griefs, nor as I had borne the death of my father, for then the soul was buried in peace, not delivered over to pain. What she suffered then was only a shock to nature.' As always, she analysed her feelings in order to discern wherein her present suffering differed from that which she had known earlier. Her present suffering was intense, and she felt every pang of it – but she bore it with a strength that was not her own. This was the conclusion she came to. 'These sufferings were impressed on me by God Himself, as in Jesus Christ; He suffered as God and man; in short, God-Man, suffering and rejoicing, without the beatitude diminishing anything of the pain, or the pain interrupting or altering the perfect beatitude.'

The most learned theologian could scarcely have expressed it better than the widow who, having given away the bulk of her personal fortune, was doing jobs of sweeping and washing in the very establishment her wealth was supporting. She managed the sweeping without much difficulty. 'What troubled me most was that I had never done washing, and it was necessary for me to wash all the linen of the sacristy . . . I spoiled everything!' she added ruefully. She had to request one of the servants she had brought with her, now under the authority of the Superior, to help her out.

When her domestic duties and the religious services of the House did not claim her attention she retreated to her room, and there she replied to the denunciatory letters she was receiving. She was evidently better at writing than at washing, for those letters had a surprising effect on the recipients, turning them in her favour, as she learned later.

For her the one comforting factor in those bewildering days was that Father La Combe had been appointed by the Bishop of Geneva to be her spiritual director. 'He is a man enlightened by God, and understands well the ways of the spirit,' the Bishop had said, adding with a flash of insight, 'and he has a singular gift for calming souls.' Perhaps he saw that that gift would be needed in her case. It was a relief to her to have this authorised connection with the only person in the neighbourhood whom she knew and could trust. From time to time Father La Combe travelled from Thonon to Gex to see her, and on one occasion walked all night in response to an urgent summons from the Sisters. Madame Guyon had been taken ill, it appeared that she was dying, and the doctors could do nothing for her. They begged him to come immediately, and receive her confession, before it was too late.

'But as soon as he entered the house, without my knowing it, my pains were alleviated. And when he came into my room and blessed me, with his hands on my head, I was perfectly cured. . . . The doctors were so surprised that they did not know how to account for my cure. Being Protestants,' she added artlessly, 'they were unable to recognise a miracle.'

Whatever may have been the view of the Protestant doctors, she was not alone in thinking that Father La Combe had been the means of working a miracle.

'My miraculous cure was written about to Paris, and made a great sensation. . . . Almost all the persons then in repute for holiness wrote to me. The Demoiselles of Paris, who were renowned for good works, congratulated me.' One wealthy lady wrote to her, sending a large gift of money with the assurance that more would follow whenever she chose to apply for it. So the tide of opinion was turning in her favour. 'At Paris they talked only of the sacrifice I had made. All approved and praised my action, so that they wanted an account of it printed, together with the miracle which had taken place. I do not know who prevented it.'

The probability is that Father de la Mothe had a hand in preventing the publication of that pamphlet eulogising his sister, just as he was behind the proposal that she should relinquish her rights to her property in favour of her children, giving power of attorney to relatives, and retaining only an annuity for herself. She was in the New Catholics' House in Gex when the suggestion reached her. She read through the legal documents that had been prepared, and although there were clauses inserted wholly to her disadvantage, they did not worry her. In her guilelessness she did not even notice them. She had taken the vow of poverty, had desired to be conformed to her Master, and she had meant what she said – and God had accepted her vow. She knew what she had to do. With the stroke of a pen as she signed her name to the document, she who had been rich became poor – so poor that on one occasion all she had to give to a beggar was some buttons.

Poverty she had asked for, and nakedness and stripping. They were to follow. She believed herself ready for them, anticipating sufferings of a general nature without realising the means by which they would come. If she had known the form in which they would be inflicted, she would have shrunk

from them. One of God's many mercies is that the future is
veiled.

*   *   *

The habit of a nun, it is generally agreed, is not one designed
to set off feminine charms, but rather the reverse, and it
usually succeeds in its purpose. However, there are some
faces, especially when young and fresh, which are so
moulded by nature that even the habit of a nun cannot
conceal their beauty, and there was one such face which fell
into that category in the New Catholic convent in Gex. The
young novice who owned it caught the eye of the ecclesiastical
gentleman who heard confessions in the House, and the more
she caught his eye, the more confessions he encouraged her to
make. 'The little Bishop', as he was called behind his back,
then set out to persuade her that what she needed was a private
retreat, which he offered to conduct for her personally.

   What it would all have led to must be left to the
imagination, for that is as far as it got, much to the chagrin of
'the little Bishop'. Things would have gone for him just as he
planned had it not been for the influence of that woman from
Paris – Madame Guyon. It was she who observed what was
happening, got the ear of the young novice, started teaching
her to pray personally in addition to repeating the usual
offices, and persuaded her not to enter into a private retreat
with him, but rather to wait for Father La Combe. He was
due to arrive shortly for the purpose of conducting retreats in
the establishment.

   'Our Lord gave her such blessing in her prayers that this
girl gave herself to God in earnest and with all her heart. The
retreat completed the victory. Now, as she apparently
recognised that to connect herself with that ecclesiastic was
something imperfect, she was more reserved,' observed
Madame Guyon, adding that the little Bishop was very put
out over the whole affair, and very embittered against her
and Father La Combe. There was little enough he could do
to regain control over the young novice, but there was quite a

lot he could do to make things uncomfortable for Madame Guyon.

It was an awkward situation for her since she, like everyone else, went to him for confession, and the difficulty was that she had so little to confess. This amazed him, but as she explained, her present manner of life provided few opportunities for committing faults. There was one sin of her past life for which she could not forgive herself, though she had confessed it before, but when she told him of it he was not satisfied. She must be hiding something. He jeered at her covertly, and went so far as to preach against her, without actually mentioning her name. There were some people who were so proud that instead of confessing gross sins, they confessed only peccadilloes, he said, and then repeated word for word what she had said in the confessional box. Such trivial matters! Eventually Madame Guyon wrote to Father La Combe and asked him if it would be all right to confess some of her past sins, just to satisfy the little Bishop.

Father La Combe's reply in the negative was prompt and unequivocal. 'He told me, no! That I should take great care not to confess them except as past, and that in confession the utmost sincerity was needed.' The little Bishop continued dissatisfied, and said so.

He was not the only enemy she made while in the convent at Gex. Female hearts, she observed, even in such secluded places, can prove very vulnerable. Marriage being out of the question, the instinctive desire for relationship with a man can take another form, apparently entirely spiritual. Madame Guyon recognised this. She had read in St. Francis de Sales' *Devout Life* the warning to discern between true and vain friendships, the danger of mistaking the one for the other, and the need to be on one's guard. 'This is particularly true when they are contracted between persons of opposite sexes, under no matter what pretext, for Satan very often touches those that love. They begin with virtuous love, but if they are not very prudent fond love will begin to insert itself, then sensual love, and afterwards carnal love.' This she had read and noted, so when one of the nuns confided in her that God had revealed to her that Father La Combe was a saint, something in the woman's attitude disturbed her.

'He is a saint, and I am going to take a vow to obey him in everything,' the nun went on ardently, and was evidently on the verge of pronouncing the vow, then and there, but Madame Guyon stopped her.

'You mustn't do that!' she said. 'These things cannot be undertaken lightly – besides, it would not be right to do it without first consulting the person concerned, to find out whether or not he would accept the responsibility.'

This seemed reasonable, and the nun agreed to write to Father La Combe, affirming that God had revealed to her that he was a saint, and that she wanted to take a vow of obedience to him.

'I believe she was then quite sincere, for she had ups and downs of weakness, which are common enough to our sex and ought to make us very humble,' wrote Madame Guyon later. 'Father La Combe answered her quickly, and she showed me the letter. He told her she should never make a vow to obey any man; that he would never be her adviser; that the person who is suitable at one time is not so in another, and that as for himself, he had never received such a vow from anyone, and never would; that it was even forbidden him by their rules.' He added, however, that he would serve her to the best of his ability, and as he was coming to Gex in the near future to conduct retreats he would have a talk with her.

The outcome of that conversation was disastrous. The nun flew into a rage at what he said to her, went to the little Bishop with her grievances, and together they joined forces to bring about the downfall of both Madame Guyon and Father La Combe.

They started on Father La Combe. The nun asked him to preach a sermon on the inner life, which he did, taking as his text, 'The beauty of the King's daughter comes from within.'

He explained what the inner life is, and how one should act from it. When he had finished the little Bishop angrily asserted that it was preached against him, and had been done deliberately to offend him.

Father La Combe assured him that it was not so, and that he had already preached the same sermon in a number of other places. As it happened, being a methodical man, he had kept a list of places where he preached it on the sermon notes, and so was able to produce them on the spot, as evidence. Instead of being appeased the little Bishop was further infuriated. Father La Combe, well instructed in humility, quietly got down on his knees without saying a word, and while the little Bishop raved on remained there with head bowed. It won for him the approval of most of the onlookers, enhancing his reputation for holiness, though they wisely kept quiet about it at the time. Meanwhile, the little Bishop, not content with abusing him, said his sermon was full of errors, and that he would write to Rome about it. He wanted what Father La Combe had said to be examined by the Sacred College and the Inquisition.

When the tirade was over Father La Combe rose to his feet and went on his way little realising what further trouble was brewing for him. He went to Annecy, where lived the Bishop of Geneva, as he had to see him about some affairs in Thonon. But the Bishop was not interested in affairs in Thonon. What was occupying his mind was Madame Guyon. That lady had already given a great sum of money to the New Catholics in his diocese, but she still had an income of her own, and the Bishop did not like the idea of it going elsewhere. Furthermore, the lady had some influential friends in Paris. Who could tell how much more money might be directed into the coffers of the New Catholics in Gex if only Madame Guyon could be persuaded to bind herself to them? So with the idea of keeping her permanently in Gex he had made the proposition to her that she should be installed in the House where she was residing as its Superior. She was already having a splendid influence on its inmates, he had told her – how greatly that could be extended if only she would agree to becoming Superior!

Madame Guyon had promptly rejected the idea. Very reasonably, she had pointed out that she had not even served a two-year novitiate, so how could she become Superior of a House? In any case, she was not prepared to bind herself, as she believed her vocation to be elsewhere. But the Bishop would not take no for an answer, and with the arrival of Father La Combe, whom he had appointed as her director, he thought he saw a way of making her change her mind.

'Father La Combe, it is absolutely necessary to bind Madame Guyon to give what she has to the House of Gex, and to become its Superior,' he said. 'And I want you to help me to persuade her to do so.'

'My lord, she had already told you of her vocation, both when you met her in Paris and here,' remonstrated Father La Combe. 'I don't believe she will bind herself. It is not likely that, having given up everything in the hope of going to Geneva, she should bind herself elsewhere. By doing that she would make it impossible for her to fulfil God's purposes for her. She is ready to remain with the Sisters as a lodger, if they will have her. If not, she will go to some convent, and wait there to see how God directs her.'

'My Father, I know all that,' said the Bishop impatiently. 'But I also know that she is very obedient. You are her director, and if you instruct her to do it, she will obey.'

'All the more reason, since she is so obedient, to be very cautious how one commands her,' retorted Father La Combe. 'It is not likely that I will urge a foreign lady, who now has only the little income she has reserved for herself, to give that to a House which has not yet been founded. Which, perhaps, never will be founded! If this House fails, on what will the lady live? Shall she go to the almshouses?'

The Bishop got really angry at this. 'All these reasons are good for nothing,' he snapped. 'If you don't make the lady do it, I will excommunicate you.'

Father La Combe was taken by surprise. He knew the rules of the interdict, and that the Bishop was going beyond his measure. But he answered readily enough that whatever happened, he would rather die than do anything against his honour and his conscience, and bowed himself out. He left behind him an infuriated man in whom the little Bishop in Gex could find inflammable material on which to work.

Extracts from 'The Nativity'

But I am poor; oblation I have none
None for a Saviour, but Himself alone:
Whate'er I render Thee, from Thee it came:
And, if I give my body to the flame,
My patience, love, energy divine,
Of heart and soul and spirit, all are Thine;
Ah, vain attempt to expunge the mighty score!
The more I pay, I owe Thee still the more.

Upon my meanness, poverty, and guilt,
The trophy of Thy glory shall be built;
My self-disdain shall be th' unshaken base,
And my deformity its fairest grace;
For destitute of good and rich in ill,
Must be my state and my description still.

Jeanne de la Mothe Guyon

6

Thonon to Turin

Madame Guyon was not happy in Gex. If personal inclination had prevailed she would have remained in Thonon with her daughter in the Ursuline convent, and not returned to Gex at all. Her obedience to ecclesiastical authority had taken her there in the first place, rather than to Geneva itself, and then La Combe's advice to stay there until God showed her, perhaps through circumstances, that she should move away, had confirmed her in doing so. The harshness with which she was treated by the nuns, allied to some strange experiences of occult forces, with noises in her room at night, and once a mental picture of Satan himself, his face horrible in a bluish light, made the place sufficiently uncongenial for her to want to get away from it. However, that very fact was, for her, a reason for staying. Also, there was the apparent need to give moral and spiritual support to the young nun who was being harassed by the little Bishop. She therefore made no attempt to move until the circumstantial guidance came to which La Combe had referred.

It came in the form of two letters. One was from La Combe himself, written immediately after his interview with the Bishop of Geneva, telling her exactly what had passed between them, warning her what to expect that she might act accordingly. The other, providentially, came from the Ursulines in Thonon, urging her to come, as the sister who was looking after her little daughter was ill. This second letter was all that she needed. Showing it to the nuns she announced her intention of going at once, and there were obviously no grounds on which they could stop her. Thus she was extricated from the New Catholics at Gex, and never returned.

Meanwhile, Father La Combe had been summoned to Rome. His doctrine was being called into question. He had become widely known in the region of Thonon for his powerful preaching, and for the influence of the missions he held. That was all very well, but now there were suggestions that what he was saying might be heretical, and due examination of it must be made. The very day after Madame Guyon arrived at the convent of the Ursulines in Thonon, he left the city, first to preach the Lenten sermons in the Valley of Aost, then to proceed to Rome. He managed to fit in a visit to her, however, to warn her that trouble was brewing, and that he himself would not be at hand to stand by her. He was sorry to leave her in a strange country without help at such a time, he told her.

What he did not tell her was that rumours were being spread about his association with her, that it was insinuated they were having illicit relations under the cloak of religion. He had not missed the covert glances and remarks dropped by one or two of the ecclesiastics who he knew disliked him, and who resented his popularity as a preacher. In one way he was not sorry to be going to Rome. At any rate he could not be suspected of carrying on with a woman and meeting her privately if he were so far away. But he wondered how she would feel, left alone to face the music.

Her reaction to the unexpected information of his immediate departure for Rome was reassuring. On the human level it must have been a disagreeable shock to her, especially when he explained that he might be detained there for a very long time. He was undoubtedly her closest friend in the neighbourhood, and the only one to whom she could turn for advice. But she showed neither alarm nor dismay. When God withdrew human supports, she said, she managed very well, for He did not withdraw His mercy. In fact, if they never met again, she would not be upset, she assured him. God's will was what mattered. If it was His will they should be separated, she not only acquiesced to it, but accepted it gladly. He could go to Rome with an easy mind on that score. So they parted, conscious that for each of them the way ahead was likely to be a difficult one.

As things worked out, their apprehensions over La Combe

proved groundless. So far from being condemned, his doctrine was praised at Rome. 'He was received with so much honour, and his doctrine so esteemed that the Sacred Congregation did him the honour of taking his views on certain points of doctrine, and found them so sound and clear that it followed them.' When he eventually returned to Thonon he was cleared of all fault by Rome. He could continue his activities of conducting missions and receiving confessions as before, to the disappointment of those who had been spreading reports about his heresies.

For her, things did not go so smoothly. The Bishop and her half-brother, Father de la Mothe, ganged up to get her back to Gex, she knew that the little Bishop was implying that she had had a lesbian relationship with the young nun there, and in addition, her letters were being intercepted. For months she was without the remittances due to her, and this could have been serious, but for some encouraging evidences of God's overruling. She related some of them to Father La Combe, on his return from Rome.

'After having been many months without any news of my papers, and when people even pressed me to write, blaming me for my indifference, an invisible hand held me back . . .' It was an exercise in patience, although action would have been easier. But she waited, and, 'Some time after I received a letter from our domestic ecclesiastic, telling me he was ordered to come and see me, and bring my papers.'

There were other occasions, too, when she was conscious of God's hand in her affairs. 'I had sent to me from Paris a considerable package for my daughter. It was lost on the lake, and I could get no news of it, but I gave myself no trouble. I believed still it would be found. At the end of three months a person had it brought to us. It was found – the house of a poor man. He had not opened it, and did not know who had brought it there.

'Once when I had sent for all the money which had to supply my wants for an entire year, the person who had been to cash the letter of exchange, having placed the money in two bags on a horse, forgot that it was there, and gave his horse to a boy to lead. He let the money fall from the horse in the middle of the market-place of Geneva. I arrived at that moment, coming from the other side, and having got out of my litter, the first thing I found was the money, over which I walked; and what is surprising is that, though there was a great crowd on that spot, no one had seen it. Many similar things happened to me, but I won't mention them all, for fear of becoming tedious.'

Here in Thonon she was often ill, at one period for about eight months on end. It was during those times of physical weakness, often lying prostrate on her bed, that she entered into new dimensions of spiritual experience, interpreting them as she understood them. She arrived at all her conclusions in this way. As she expressed it:

'Our Lord instructed me by experience. It is the way He has always acted with me. He has not enlightened me by illumination and knowledge, but while making me experience the things, He has given me the understanding of what I experienced.'

Whatever may have been the reason for her veneration of the Virgin Mary when she was young, it now stemmed from the fact that through her the Child Jesus had been born. And in a spiritual sense she could relate to her, for had not Jesus Christ said that whoever did the will of His Father, the same was His mother, His brother, His sister? 'I understood also the maternity of the Holy Virgin, and in what manner we participate in her maternity . . . producing Him in souls.' This, it began to dawn on her, was to be her role – a spiritual mother.

Page after page of her autobiography deals with the flights of her spirit during those months in Thonon. The Last Supper became real to her.

'In an ineffable silence I understood the manner in which Jesus Christ communicated Himself to His intimates, and the communication of St. John on the breast of our Lord at the Last Supper. . . . It was then there was communicated to him that wonderful secret of the eternal generation of the Word, because he was rendered a participator in the ineffable intercourse of the Holy Trinity. . . . It was then he learned the difference of being "born of the flesh, of the will of man, or of the will of God".'

She learned secrets of silence. 'You made me conceive, O Divine Word, that as You are always speaking and working in a soul, although You there appear in a profound silence . . . I learned then a language unknown to me before . . .'

She had confrontations with the prince of darkness, too, as well as revelations concerning the woman in the Apocalypse, who had the moon under her feet, was encircled with the sun, had twelve stars on her head and cried in the pains of childbirth. From this she understood that the moon under her feet signified that her soul would be above the vicissitudes of mortal life, since she was surrounded by the sun, representing God Himself, and that the pregnancy indicated spiritual children, and the dragon was the Devil who would seek, unsuccessfully, to devour them. Spiritual motherhood again, with its birth-pangs and pain, and an enemy ready to attack . . .

It was during this time of constant illness that she developed the ability which was to bring her into the public eye, and preserve her name for posterity. She started to write.

For several years she had written poetry, on and off, but this was different. She told Father La Combe that she felt strongly urged to write, and he told her the same thought had been impressed upon him. But what did she want to write? he asked. She had no idea, she answered. So he told her to write as the spirit moved her, and that is what she did. Words poured from her pen without any reflection on her part, and within a short time she had written a whole treatise on three classes of souls, as she saw them – souls that have turned to God and known His life within them, but who respond in varying degrees of fervour. With the analogy of streams and rivers, she likened some to the slow and sluggish that meander along and get nowhere, some to those that flow more rapidly, gathering rivulets to join their progress towards the ocean, and some to mighty torrents that pour down with an impetuosity that nothing can hinder. When she had finished writing, she thought no more of it. She just knew that she felt relieved, and her health improved.

However, La Combe demanded that she continue writing. Let her write to him everything that came to mind, all her experiences, the things that had happened to her, her spiritual growth. He was frequently away conducting missions, so he could not see her often, and as her spiritual director he wanted to know how she was getting on. It is possible that he not only wanted to learn from her but also to rectify what might be wrong thinking! There were times when the two of them got on each other's nerves. Something she told him 'irritated him against me several days. When I told him anything, this produced in him disgust for me and alienation.' She put this down to his spiritual immaturity, and as she felt as great a responsibility for his soul as he felt for hers, she 'suffered a martyrdom exceeding anything that can be told, and which has been very protracted'. After all, he might have been appointed her spiritual director by the Bishop, and this she gladly accepted, but they both of them took the view that she was, to him, his mother in Christ. And as such, she watched for his soul.

'I had so strong an instinct for his perfection, and to see him die to himself, that I would have wished him all the ills imaginable, far from pitying him.' Death to self was the only way to perfection, and dying could be painful, but it was necessary. 'When he was not faithful, or took things so as to nourish the self-life, I felt myself devoured . . .'

By and large, however, they got on very well, for they both had the same object in view – perfect union with God, and what she referred to as 'annihilation' of the self-life in order that His will might have unhindered sway.

Although their influence in the neighbourhood was mainly through their teaching, they were also noted for improving social conditions. Madame Guyon had always visited and helped the poor in practical ways, and when she was well enough she continued these activities. But it was during one of her periods of sickness that Father La Combe, stirred to action by what he saw of the plight of the poor, conceived the idea of establishing a little hospital for them. He got the cooperation of the local authorities to the extent of obtaining from them the use of some rooms they did not require, and Madame Guyon, as soon as she heard about it, donated some beds. Others followed her example, and in a very short space of time the hospital was a going concern, with twelve beds, and a voluntary staff of workers to run it. At this point Madame Guyon's flair for compounding ointments proved of very practical value. She taught the staff how to make them, and instructed them to sell them to the rich, so obtaining an income for the running of the hospital, while the poor who needed them were to receive them free of charge.

'The Dames of Charity were so well disposed that through their charity, and the care of the nuns, this hospital is very well maintained,' she wrote years later. 'Those Dames formed a union also to provide for the sick who could not go to the hospital, and I gave them some little rules I had observed when in France. They have kept this up with love and charity.' Then followed a simple note which revealed the centrality of Christ in her thinking, and the significance with which she regarded dates and anniversaries. 'We had also the devotion to cause every twenty-fifth of the month a service of blessing to be celebrated in the chapel of the Congregation, which is dedicated to the Holy Child Jesus; and for this we gave a complete outfit to the chapel.'

The effect of this quiet manifestation of charity and devotion was two-fold. It gained the approbation of the people of Thonon, but infuriated the Bishop of Geneva, who angrily told her that she was winning over everyone to her way of thinking, and that he did not want her in his diocese. The Prioress of the Ursulines who had become her friend had a hard time of it at his hands – or, to be more accurate, his tongue. And as Madame Guyon was so often ill, and the physicians said the proximity of the convent to the waters of the lake was bad for her, she decided to move away to a more secluded spot.

'I left the Ursulines, and a house at a distance from the lake was sought for me. The only empty one available had every appearance of the utmost poverty. There was no chimney except in the kitchen, through which we had to pass to reach the room. I took my daughter with me, and gave the largest room to her and the maid who attended her. I settled in a little hole with some straw, which I went up to by a wooden ladder. As I had no furniture but our bedsteads, which were white, I bought some rush-seated chairs, with plates and dishes of earthenware and wood.

'Never have I tasted such contentment as I found in this little spot,' she continued, remembering vividly the simplicity of those days. 'It seemed to me so in harmony with Jesus Christ. I relished everything better on wood than on silver. I can say that I have never tasted an equal pleasure to that in this poor and solitary little place where I lived. I was happier than kings!' Her companions were her little daughter, a lively, adaptable child, and her maid.

This young woman, the maid, had been brought to Thonon by a relative of Madame Guyon who had come from Paris to visit her, and the girl remained in Madame Guyon's employ. Madame Guyon always believed that God had inspired that visit for the sole purpose of bringing the girl to her. She was to prove a loyal and devoted servant and companion through all the trials that lay ahead.

The trials were soon encountered. The peace of the tiny home, not much better than a hovel, was shattered when rioters came, throwing stones through the windows, shouting abuse, and then one night tearing up all the trellis work in the little garden that had been so carefully put in order, overturning pots and plants, leaving it looking as though an invading army had gone through it.

She learned later who had set the rioters on to these unprovoked assaults – the little Bishop at Gex. However, there was nothing she could do about it. There was no civil authority to which she could turn for help or protection, for the Bishop himself had made it quite plain that he did not want her any longer in his diocese. In any case, she was always reluctant to plead for help from man, and at this time she seemed benumbed. 'I was so lost that I could neither see nor regard anything, taking all that came as from the hand of God. During all this time I never felt grief or regret at what I had done in giving up all.' Nor was she plagued with fears that she might have made a mistake. She had committed her way to God, and was confident that He had her affairs in hand.

So it proved to be. Unknown to her, someone was working quietly on her behalf, away in Italy. The godly Marquise de Prunai, sister of the chief State Secretary, living in the city of Turin, had heard about her and the difficulties she was encountering, and sent her a warm invitation to come and stay with her. Then she felt impelled by a superior power, God Himself she believed, to take further action. She obtained a *lettre de cachet* instructing Madame Guyon, accompanied by Father La Combe, to proceed to Turin.

This came as a complete surprise to both of them, but its arrival was certainly opportune as far as Madame Guyon was concerned. They both saw in it the hand of God, and accepted it unhesitatingly.

Knowing the rumours that were being spread about them, however, they took the precaution of ensuring that they did not travel together unaccompanied. A monk who had been teaching theology, and a boy Madame Guyon had brought from France and had trained as a tailor, went with them. The men rode on horses, Madame Guyon and her little girl and the maid in a litter. Nothing could have been more decorous, since the presence of an ecclesiastic travelling as escort was sufficient to lend an air of respectability to any company.

So they arrived in Turin. Once again she had been extricated from a situation in which she was helplessly entangled – but once again it was seen to be Father La Combe who was with her, and the rumours linking their names together persisted. She had prayed for ignominy and shame, and she was to get what she had asked for.

Prayer is the key of perfectness and of supreme well-being. It is the effectual means of delivering us from all vices and of acquiring all virtues; for the great means of becoming perfect is to walk in the presence of God. This He said Himself, 'Walk in My presence, and be perfect.' (Gen. 18.1) 'Tis prayer alone that can give you this presence, and that can give it you continually . . .

This is not the prayer of the head, but the prayer of the heart. It is not a prayer of thought only, because the spirit of man is so bounded that while he thinks on one thing he cannot think on another; but it is the prayer of the heart, which is not at all interrupted by all the occupations of the mind; nothing but irregular affections can interrupt the prayer of the heart . . .

Jeanne de la Mothe Guyon, from "A Method of Prayer"

7

Exodus from Grenoble

The Marquise de Prunai spoke very little French. She had heard about Madame Guyon, and the harsh treatment she had received in Gex and Thonon, and her heart had been touched. The circumstances of her own life had been similar in some respects, for she, too, had been left a widow in her twenties, and had decided against remarrying in order that she could devote herself, devotionally and practically, to religious exercises. She was glad to welcome into her home this Frenchwoman whose reputation for piety, and an unusual spirituality, had reached her.

But Madame Guyon spoke very little Italian. Furthermore, she was exhausted after the strain of the past months, and could not adapt quickly to her new situation. She was often silent, and sometimes felt so ill that she took to her bed. Then her elder son arrived, with news of her mother-in-law's death and complications that had arisen regarding her property. Madame Guyon did not divulge what were her feelings towards the son who had been so heartlessly estranged from her when a child. She merely wrote in her autobiography, 'My elder son came to see me on the subject of my mother-in-law's death, which was a very serious addition to my crosses; but after we had heard all his reasons – seeing without me they had sold all the movables, elected guardians, and settled everything independently of me – I was quite useless.'

The marquise, not surprisingly, found it hard to understand her guest. She seemed spiritless and rather stupid. The only person who appeared to have any influence over her was Father La Combe, who had left her in Turin and gone on to Verceil, thirty or forty miles away, at the invitation of the Bishop there. The marquise began to lose patience.

For Madame Guyon, a stranger in a strange land, Father La Combe was again the only one with whom she felt she could communicate freely. She wrote to him frequently, and he came to Turin occasionally, as her spiritual director. It came as an unpleasant shock, like a douche of cold water, to find that time and time again he apparently failed to understand her. When she turned to him for guidance as to what she should do, he told her he had no light on the matter. She must do what she believed to be right. They often disagreed, usually in their assessment of others. Limited as she was, with no household or social responsibilities, with inadequate language and generally poor health, she became excessively concerned about the spiritual condition of those whom she met, and who went to him for confession. When she told him that this one and that one was still full of SELF, he would accuse her of pride, and rash judgment, while she would grieve that he was so lacking in discernment. They knew each other well enough, and had sufficient humour to agree that if their association had been the natural one of which their detractors accused them, it would have broken up long ago.

'He who to everyone else was gentle, often had for me an extreme hardness,' she wrote. It pained her, but through it all she believed it was the will of God, that she might be left with no support but in God Himself. As for Father La Combe, he found that when he was at odds with her, he was uneasy. It interrupted his communion with God.

'When I am well with God I am well with you, and as soon as I am ill with God I am ill with you,' he told her more than once. The deep union of spirit they had always known was not without its testings.

Her spiritual relationship with La Combe was not the only experience of those months in Italy. Although she felt unusually helpless, 'childlike' as she expressed it, she found to her own surprise that when confronted with people who had a particular need, unknown to themselves, she could put her finger on it. '. . . Our Lord made me utter oracles; for when it was a question of helping anyone, or of anything our Lord wished for me, He gave me a divine strength.' Discernment of spirits was being given to her, and the time for the exercise of it was soon to come. As so often happens, guidance came as the result of outward events.

The marquise announced that she had to leave Turin for her estate in the country. This threw Madame Guyon into a state of uncertainty. What should she do? What about her daughter's education if she took her to the marquise's place in the country? She had to make a decision, but seemed unable to do so until one day, quite unexpectedly, Father La Combe arrived from Verceil, and for once he took a determined line with her. He told her what to do. Speaking quite firmly, he said she was to leave Turin immediately, and proceed to Paris.

To Paris! To the place where Father de la Mothe had been spreading rumours about her, asserting that she was running after Father La Combe, that she had left home on account of him, and that they had been seen in all sorts of compromising situations together! But such was her state of bewilderment and personal indecision that without a demur she started making preparations to leave Turin with her little daughter and the maid, the very next day.

Father La Combe accompanied her, much against his own will (he did not want to give occasion for any more scandals about him and this lady) but because the Father Provincial of Turin ordered him to. 'She can't be allowed to travel through those mountains without someone she knows to accompany her – especially as she has her child to look after. You must go with her,' he said. 'Go with her as far as Grenoble. She'll be in her own country then. You can leave her there, and come back here immediately.' So off they went, arrived safely in Grenoble, a town a couple of hundred miles south of Geneva, and there La Combe left her with a friend who lived there. But he spoke no more of her going on to Paris.

'I believe God has a work for you to do here,' he told her. 'I think you should remain here.' Accommodation was found for her in a widow's home, her little girl, about whose lack of a suitable French education she had been worried, was placed in a convent, and she herself settled down to what she expected to be a quiet and secluded life. It was what she always longed for.

But solitude did not last long. Unknown to herself, her reputation had gone before her, and when it was known she had come to Grenoble the city was agog with the news. She was actually here, this wealthy widow who had given away a fortune, helped to found a hospital in Thonon, and whose personal conversations with a variety of people were said to have brought them in touch with God! To her great surprise she started receiving calls from those who had heard of her, and wished to meet her. Then it was that she realised what was happening to her.

'I at once became aware of a gift of God, which had been communicated to me without my understanding it, namely, the discernment of spirits, and the giving to each what was suitable to him. I discerned the state of the souls of the persons who spoke to me, and that with such facility that they were astonished and said one to the other that I gave each that of which he was in need.

'It was You, O my God, who did all these things!

'They sent each other to me. It reached such a point that ordinarily from six in the morning till eight in the evening I was occupied in speaking of God. People came from all sides, from far and near – monks, priests, men of the world, girls, women and widows – all came, the one after the other, and God gave me wherewith to satisfy all in an admirable manner, without my taking any thought, or paying any attention to it.'

The effect of what she said to them, sometimes even her silences, was evident.

'God gave them great graces and worked marvellous changes . . . I saw monks of different orders and priests of merit, to whom our Lord gave great graces; and God gave grace to all, without exception – at least, to all who came in good faith.'

Inevitably there were some who did not come in good faith. One day a little group came to catch her out in her words. Although she did not know who they were, or what were their motives, she found herself unable to say anything to them, and they eventually went off to report that the woman was quite stupid, she hadn't a thing to say. Some time later one of her friends arrived in a hurry, and exclaimed, 'Oh, I couldn't get here soon enough! I wanted to warn you not to say anything to those people. They were sent to spy on you.'

'Our Lord has been beforehand with your kindness,' replied Madame Guyon with a twinkle. 'I wasn't able to say a word to them!'

She was in Grenoble for about two years, and it was a golden period in her life. She was the centre of a spiritual revival, the effects of which were evident in many circles of society.

'I have never in my life had so much consolation in seeing in that little town so many good souls who vied with each other in giving themselves to God with their whole heart. There were young girls of twelve or thirteen years of age, who worked all day in silence in order to converse with God. As they were poor girls, those who knew how to read out something to those who could not. It was a revival of the innocence of the early Christians.

'There was a poor washerwoman who had five children and a husband paralysed in the right arm, but more halt in his spirit than in his body; he had no strength except to beat her. Nevertheless this poor woman, with the sweetness of an angel, endured it all, and gained subsistence for that man and her five children. This woman had a wonderful gift of prayer, preserving the presence of God and equanimity in the greatest miseries and poverty.'

It was not only among the lower classes of society that Madame Guyon's emphasis on personal and private prayer was having its effect. Among the members of the upper classes in Grenoble, too, were many who came to her, and among them one, a counsellor of the Parliament, who remained her staunch friend and who was instrumental in bringing her teaching before a much wider public. It all happened in quite a casual way. He came to see her one day, noticed a manuscript entitled *A Method of Prayer* on her table, and glancing through it, asked if he might borrow it. She had written it months before, she told him, and used it to help some of the people who came to her. He brought it back to her a short time later, telling her that he had shown it to several of his friends, all of whom wanted a copy of it, and he asked her permission to have it printed. Nothing could be printed without royal consent, but this approbation was duly obtained, and she was asked to write a preface to it. So her first book was published, and the first edition ran out in no time. Some of the monks she had been in touch with took fifteen hundred copies outright, and the little publication found its way into the hands of people she had never heard of, and to places she never expected to visit. It was a great success.

No one could have foreseen the troubles it would cause her. Private and personal prayer was seen by some as a threat to the Establishment. There is something almost ludicrous in the fact that the trouble started in Grenoble, not because of the little book, but because of the washerwoman who was known to pray.

It came about in this way. The washerwoman had two friends, one the wife of a shopkeeper, the other of a locksmith, and when there was an opportunity they used to read aloud to her from the Bible. They were amazed at her grasp of what she heard, of the deep insight she had into the

Scriptures that were read to her, and her eloquence in speaking of it. Somehow this reached the ears of a group of monks of a certain order who were all against private prayer.

'These monks sent for this woman, and threatened her if she would not give up prayer, saying it was only for monks, and that she was very audacious to use prayer. She answered them – or, rather, He who taught her, for she was in herself very ignorant – that our Lord had told all to pray; and that He had said, "I say unto you *all*," not specifying either priests of monks; that without prayer she could never support the crosses, nor the poverty she was in; that she had formerly been without prayer, and she was a demon; and that since she used it, she had loved God with all her heart; and therefore to give up prayer was to renounce her salvation, which she never could do.

'She added, let them take twenty persons who have never used prayer, and twenty of those who use it; then, said she, make yourselves acquainted with their lives, and you will see if you have reason in condemning prayer.'

Such a reasonable argument infuriated the monks. They threatened her that she should be refused absolution unless she promised to give up praying. Even that did not shake her. The Lord was her Master, she said, and He would communicate with her in whatever way He pleased.

Highly incensed, they refused her absolution, went on to abuse a tailor who was known as a very godly man and who also prayed, then demanded that all books on prayer should be brought out and burned. They made a great bonfire of them in a public square. They were very pleased with themselves over this. Then they went too far. A Father of the Oratory, well-known in the town and well-liked, was known to pray at evening, and on Sundays made a short and fervent prayer which helped others to learn how to pray, too. The monks beat him up.

That was too much for the townsfolk. If the monks went around terrifying members of the lower orders, it did not matter much, but to attack with sticks a Father of the Oratory! Public opinion was aroused to such an extent that the authorities had to do something about it. They sent for the Bishop of Geneva, who came and protested from the pulpit that he had no part in what had happened, that the monks, in their false zeal, had gone beyond their measure. Things quietened down after that for a time, but inevitably word got around that something was happening in Grenoble. People were praying privately.

Meanwhile, Madame Guyon was brought in touch with some monks of the very order that had created the sensation by their burning of books and beating of prelates. It started with the visit a friar paid her. He had come begging for money, that being his job, but when he discovered that she was ill, he gave her some of his medicines, medicine being a sideline of his. She recovered very quickly, and when they got into conversation, she, as usual, spoke about God, and in a very short time he was explaining to her that he did have a love for God, but that he was so busy he hadn't the time to develop it.

We don't need *time* to love God, she explained. We can love Him and think of Him, whatever we are doing. The friar's attention was arrested. There was that about her which had the same effect on him as on the many others that she met – something which quickened the desire for the spiritual life that she obviously enjoyed. He opened up, confiding in her his feelings, and as she talked to him, gently reminding him of the simplicity of speaking to God in the heart, his spirits revived, and he eventually left her saying, 'You are my true mother.' There were many who called her that, confirming the vision she had had in which she had been told she would be the spiritual mother of multitudes.

The friar did not keep quiet about what had happened. Back in the House to which he was attached, he told some of the monks there about his experience, and they, too, went to Madame Guyon. This reached the ears of the Superior of the

House, and the Master of the novices. That there was an improvement in the dispositions and general behaviour of the monks in question they could not deny, but they were annoyed that it should all have come about through a woman.

'They were vexed that a woman, they said, should be so sought after . . . they only had scorn for the gift which was contained in so miserable a vessel, in place of esteeming only God and His grace, without regard to the baseness of the subject in which he pours it out.'

However, as Madame Guyon gave a great deal to charity, the Superior of the House eventually came to thank her, and in talking with her was so completely won over that he distributed quantities of her little book, for which he and the monks paid themselves. 'It was, then, monks of this same order of whom our Lord made use to establish prayer in I know not how many places, and they carried a hundred times more books on prayer into the places where they went than their brothers had burnt. God appears to me wonderful in these things.'

Meanwhile her personal conversations continued. Some of the confessors complained that their penitents confided more in her than in themselves, while others applauded her. 'It was here one might easily see the difference between those confessors who sought only God in the conduct of souls, and those who sought themselves. The former used to come to see me, and were delighted with the graces which God bestowed on their penitents, without paying attention to the channel of which He made use. The others, on the contrary, secretly moved to stir up the town against me.' Some came to her to argue with her on theological matters, of which she confessed herself to be ignorant. 'Although they were matters beyond my scope, our Lord made me answer with as much correctness as if I had studied them all my life. . . . They went away not only convinced and satisfied, but smitten by God's love.'

When night came and her stream of visitors ceased, she

started writing. She was soaking herself in the Scriptures now, and could not refrain from passing on what she discovered.

'I had no book except the Bible, and that alone I used without searching for anything. When, in writing on the Old Testament, I took passages from the New to support what I was saying, it was not that I sought them out but they were given to me at the same time as the explanation . . . and exactly the same with the New Testament.

'I wrote with incredible quickness, for the hand could hardly follow the spirit that dictated.' It took the copyist five days to copy what she wrote in a single night. A flow of inner strength sustained her in a remarkable way during that period in Grenoble. She mentioned having written a commentary on the Song of Solomon in a day and a half, in addition to interviewing the usual flow of visitors. She was becoming known as a writer as well as a spiritual counsellor, and among her other activities was the founding of another hospital, on similar lines to that in Thonon.

'My enemies have made use of this subsequently to calumniate me, saying that I had spent my children's property in establishing hospitals, although the truth is that, far from having expended their money, I have even given them my own, and that these hospitals have been established merely on the capital of divine providence, which is inexhaustible.' She would have subscribed heartily to the maxim of a later age that 'God's work, done in God's way, never lacks God's supplies.'

But she was not to be left in peace in Grenoble. Rumours began to circulate, letters were received which asserted she was a sorceress, that she attracted people by magical means, that she was in league with the devil. Others whispered that she was an immoral woman, and that as for her gifts to charity, she used false money. The absurdity of the accusations could not prevent people from talking about them, and things got to such a pass that some of her friends advised her to move away from the district for a time, until the storm had subsided. Without the support of the Bishop of Geneva, in whose diocese Grenoble was situated, she was in a vulnerable position, and the Bishop would do nothing to protect her.

So where was she to go?

Gex, Thonon, Grenoble – she felt like a hot potato in them all. There was just one place where she would be welcome, and that was in Italy. Her friendship with the Marquise de Prunai had revived, and she was receiving warm invitations from her to go back to Turin, as well as from the kindly Bishop of Verceil, urging her to return to his diocese. The obvious thing was to accept this opening, so providentially made again at the time when she needed it. There was only one obstacle in the way of her accepting it.

Father La Combe was still in Verceil. If she went again into the diocese where he was living it would look as though she were running after him, and for the sake of her own reputation as well as his, she was determined to give no occasion for further gossip. So when a leading ecclesiastic suggested she should go to Marseilles, where he assured her there would be a welcome for her, and that he himself would accompany her on the long journey south, she fell in with the idea. She would leave her daughter in the convent, where her education would not suffer through further travels, she would leave the maid from Paris, who was already proving a true colleague, in charge of the child, while she herself would go on to Marseilles.

Humanly speaking, the decision was disastrous. Her little book on prayer had reached Marseilles ahead of her, and had got into the hands of the disciples of Monsieur de St. Cyran the Jansenist. The disciples of Monsieur de St. Cyran had formed one of those groups that seem to emerge from time to time in all ages and among all classes, who are violently opposed to all with whose views they do not agree. They did not agree with Madame Guyon's suggestions as to how to pray. Within hours of her arrival in Marseilles they had created such a disturbance, demanding that the Bishop should drive her away, that she found herself laughing. She remembered how, shortly before she left Grenoble, one of the girls she had helped had come to her in great distress. She had had a nightmare, in which she had seen the Devil. 'Madame Guyon is going away,' he had told the girl, 'But I'll catch her yet. I'll be ahead of her everywhere she goes, and stir things up against her.' He certainly had lost no time in Marseilles, Madame Guyon reflected wryly as she set off to see the Bishop, in response to his summons.

However, the Devil was evidently not so successful with the Bishop as with the disciples of Monsieur de St. Cyran. He proved to be quite cordial, said he had read her book and found it very good, that the disciples of Monsieur de St. Cyran were a perfect nuisance, upsetting everybody, and that by insulting her they had insulted him. He urged her to remain in his diocese, assuring her that he would protect her.

But he could not prevent anonymous letters being written to her, nor malicious rumours from Grenoble being circulated, and after a week of it she decided she could not stay on in Marseilles either. She seemed to have no alternative now but to go to the Marquise de Prunai, and hearing that she could get to Turin via Nice, she decided to go that way.

So she set off on what proved to be the worst journey she ever took in her life. It was uneventful and pleasant enough along the coast road from Marseilles to Nice, but on arrival there she learned to her dismay that she could not travel by litter north to Turin as she had expected. No muleteer was prepared to take her up through those mountains, she was told. Putting up in an inn with her two maids and the ecclesiastic who was accompanying her, she simply did not know what to do.

'I saw myself without refuge or retreat, wandering and vagabond. All the workers I saw in their little shops appeared to me happy in having a dwelling place and a refuge, and I found nothing in the world so hard for a person

like me, who naturally loved honour, as this wandering life.'
She remembered the words with which she had been
impressed, spoken by Jesus Christ, about foxes having their
holes, birds their nests, but the Son of Man being without a
home, and she felt that she was partaking very acutely of
those sufferings. She had been prepared for ignominy, but
that did not save her from the sense of shame that accompanied it. As she walked through the streets and markets of
Nice, by the sparkling blue waters of the Mediterranean, she
thought she knew the depth of the bitterness of homelessness.
But worse was to follow.

She was told, unexpectedly, of a way whereby she could
reach the Marquise. 'A small sloop is going to Genoa
tomorrow. It will only take a day to get there,' she was told,
'and as it passes by Savona you can be landed there if you
like. It will be easy for you to get a litter in Savona to take you
to Turin.'

The little party boarded the sloop with their baggage, and
as they sailed away Madame Guyon found herself longing
for: 'A little hole in a rock, to place myself there and to live
separated from all creatures. I pictured to myself that a
desert island would have ended all my disgraces ...' When a
storm arose, and the others were crying out with fear, she was
quite calm and intrepid. They could not understand it, and
perhaps gave her credit for a faith she could not, in all
honesty, have claimed at that time. It was her longing to be
done with life, to be engulfed by the sea, that made her so
indifferent to the danger they were in.

Instead of the voyage taking a day, as had been claimed,
they were on that sloop for eleven days, battered by the wind
and waves. They could not disembark at Savona, and had to
go on to Genoa, and here they encountered storms of a
different nature. The Genonese, being Italian, did not like
the French, who had bombarded their city a few months
previously. The arrival of a Frenchwoman who looked like
an aristocrat, accompanied by a couple of maids and an
ecclesiastic, all of them pretty bedraggled, and none of them

speaking much Italian, aroused contempt and cupidity, but no mercy. They were jeered at, insulted, and the innkeeper who agreed to take them in charged as much per person as it would have cost for the whole party in a good hotel in Paris. Madame Guyon saw such inroads being made on her finances, that she would soon be without money – and in a country which if not actually at war with her own, was at least in a state of cold hostility.

And it was the beginning of Holy Week. Unless she could reach the haven of the Marquise's home before Good Friday, she would be stranded in Genoa for several days. The Doge had departed, and seemed to have taken all the available litters in the city with him, and she was at her wits' end when she was told of a muleteer who would convey her in his litter (at a price) as far as Verceil.

Could he go no farther? Could he not take her to the estate of the Marquise de Prunai? No! He did not know where the Marquise de Prunai lived, so that was that. He could take her to Verceil but no farther. Take it or leave it!

She had no alternative but to accept, though when she saw the evil-faced muleteer and his two lame mules, her heart sank. As for what Father La Combe's reaction would be to her unheralded arrival, right in the middle of Holy Week, with all its extra ceremonies and services, its festivals and fasts, she scarcely dared to speculate. In fact, that worried her almost more than anything now, and concern that he should be warned of her arrival made her decide to take the risk of travelling without the protection and help of the ecclesiastic. She would send him on ahead, so that he could arrive a day or two before her, and notify the Bishop who, after all, had originally invited her, that her plans had been changed, and that she was coming. The ecclesiastic, conscious of his unpopularity as a Frenchman in Italy, set off alone, while Madame Guyon and the two maids, seated in the litter, rumbled out of Genoa unescorted.

It was unconventional, to say the least. Three woman

travelling without the presence of an ecclesiastic to add respectability to their entourage, were laying themselves open to insult – and worse. Their muleteer made no attempt to disguise his scorn, and when nightfall came, instead of taking them to an inn, brought the litter to a halt outside a mill, opened the door on to a room where some men were already settling down for the night, and told them they could stay there.

'Here! In a room with those men! Certainly not!' Madame Guyon, the two maids cowering behind her, rose to her full height and indignantly refused to enter. 'Take us to an inn at once!' But the muleteer refused. He knew he had the upper hand, and intended to use it. He was going on no further, he said, and if the three women didn't want to spend the night in the mill, they could make their own way to the inn. At ten o'clock at night, therefore, the three of them, carrying their hand-baggage, stumbled out into the darkness, the muleteer shouting and jeering after them.

'I bore my humiliation with pleasure,' she wrote, adding candidly, 'but not without seeing or feeling it. But Your will, my God, and my abandonment to it, made everything easy to me.' It was in these extremities of fortune that the deep inner peace sustained her.

Mercifully, they were well received at the inn. 'Those good people did their best to refresh us from our fatigue, assuring us that the place where we had been taken was very dangerous. The next day we had again to return on foot to find the litter, the man refusing to bring it to us.' To crown it all, he refused to go on any further, and forced her to go on by post chaise, instead of in a private vehicle.

The arrival of the post chaise with its three female passengers at a frontier town was the occasion for further humiliation. The postillion drew up, as usual, at the inn, but when the mistress of the house heard he had three women as passengers, she stoutly refused to admit them. The argument that ensued between them drew a crowd, including some officers from the garrison, who heard the innkeeper assert that she would have no prostitutes in her establishment.

'She's not a prostitute,' argued the postillion. 'She's a very good woman – very religious. Her maids are respectable girls, too. You've got no reason not to take them in. Come and see them for yourself.' At last she was persuaded to do so, and as happened not infrequently, one look at Madame Guyon was sufficient to make her change her mind. She saw a demurely-clad middle-aged woman with a black hood shielding a face from which the pockmarks had subsided, still beautiful in contour, but completely devoid of make-up, and with such an expression of evident goodness that the mistress of the inn was won over.

'Come in,' she said. 'But lock yourselves in this room. If my son knows you are here he'll kill you. We had a lot of trouble here a few days ago. A bad woman murdered a very respectable man in this house, and it has cost us a lot of money. My son vowed he'd kill any other woman who lodged here, he was so angry about it. Lock yourselves in and don't make a sound. You must get away tomorrow without him seeing you.'

Thus ignominiously did they depart, and not much more dignified was their arrival at an inn at Verceil. On the eve of Good Friday unannounced guests were not very welcome, especially when they proved to be three travel-stained Frenchwomen who could speak very little Italian. The innkeeper's attitude changed when he learned that Madame Guyon was acquainted with Father La Combe, who was well known and greatly respected in the neighbourhood, but Father La Combe himself, when he met her, could not conceal his dismay. The unfortunate ecclesiastic whom she had sent on ahead had only just arrived, having had a very bad time of it on the road, so La Combe, during the busiest week in the year, suddenly found himself saddled with an added problem, and an embarrassment.

'People will say you've come here after me!' he said irritably. It was just what Madame Guyon herself feared, and she offered to leave immediately and go she knew not where, but he waved the foolish suggestion aside, and continued, 'I don't know how to tell the Bishop you've arrived. He's invited you to come three times, and you've refused, and he's stopped enquiring about you. What he'll think about your turning up like this, I don't know!' Father La Combe was obviously fed up with her, and that was the worst blow of all, as her autobiography revealed.

'It was then, it seemed to me, that I was cast out from the surface of the earth, and that all creatures were combined together to crush me. I spent the rest of the night in this inn, without being able to sleep, and without knowing what course I should be compelled to take, persecuted as I was by my enemies, and a subject of shame to my friends.'

She reached rock bottom that night. She had believed she could bear shame and ignominy when, in her ardour, she had asked for it, longing for the opportunity to prove her devotion to her God. When it came in this form, she found she had nothing to say, expect that it was the outcome of her own decision. Her eagerness to save herself from the accusation that she was running after Father La Combe, which was at the back of her decision to go to Marseilles rather than to the Marquise, had landed her in a worse situation than if she had accepted the providential opening in the first place.

However, she was not left in that state. The following day the Bishop, on learning that she had arrived, sent his niece to bring her into her own home and there, although she became seriously ill for a time, she was treated with respect and appreciation. The Bishop proved himself a true friend, and one who genuinely supported her.

'One could not be under greater obligation than I was to this good prelate. He conceived as much friendship for me as if I had been his sister, and in the midst of his continual occupation, his sole diversion was to spend a half-hour with me, speaking about God.' He wanted her to remain in his diocese, hoping she might help him to form a community there, but her ill health made that obviously impossible, and eventually, on the advice of her doctors, she decided to return to Paris.

But not before paying a visit to the Marquise de Prunai. It is worthy of note that during the short time she spent with her, she inspired and helped her hostess to found a little hospital, similar to those started in Thonon and Grenoble, passing on her recipes for simple remedies, and teaching her how to compound ointments.

In the welter of her experiences in the realms of the spirit, that brought her eventually on to the stage of world history, Madame Guyon's practical achievements were usually overlooked, not only by others, but also by herself. She referred to them almost as an afterthought in her auto-biography. 'I nearly forgot to mention that we started a little hospital . . .'

Two other occurrences of those last few weeks in Italy affected her far more deeply. One was the arrival of an affectionate letter from the Duchess of Charost, with whom she had almost completely lost touch. This renewed contact with her old friend, now living in Versailles, was a comfort as she prepared to proceed, with many misgivings, to Paris. She had little idea of how much she was to owe to that renewed contact in the years that lay ahead.

The other occurrence was of a different nature, and was to have a different outcome. It was an order to Father La Combe from the Superior of the Barnabites to proceed to Paris. The order went further. He was instructed to escort Madame Guyon to that city.

At the instigation of Father de la Mothe this arrangement was made. The reason he gave was that there was a great need in the capital for preachers of Father La Combe's calibre. It was not right that such a man should be left in Italy, where his eloquence would be wasted. Father de la Mothe further suggested that as his sister, who was in poor health, had to come to Paris, Father La Combe should be the ecclesiastic to accompany her, and so the Barnabite House in Paris, already poor, would be saved the expense of bringing him there. Once again the very thing they both wanted to avoid was thrust upon them. They were to travel together.

They arrived in Paris on the eve of St. Magdalene's Day, exactly five years after Madame Guyon had set off for Geneva.

About the same time, away in Rome, a Spanish priest named Molinos was being brought before the Inquisition.

The Joy of the Cross

Self-love no grace in sorrow sees,
Consults her own peculiar ease;
 'Tis all the bliss she knows:
But nobler aims pure Love employ;
In self-denial is her joy,
 In suffering her repose.

Jesus, Avenger of our fall . . .
Oh tell me – life is in Thy voice –
How much afflictions were Thy choice,
 And sloth and ease Thy scorn!

Thy choice and mine shall be the same;
Inspirer of that holy flame
 Which must for ever blaze!
To take the Cross and follow Thee,
Where love and duty lead, shall be
 My portion and my praise.

Jeanne de la Mothe Guyon

8

Imprisoned in Paris

The ecclesiastical climate in France, which had been electric for years, had broken in a storm at last. With the revocation of the Edict of Nantes, which had ensured religious liberty for the Huguenots, who were Protestants, these now found themselves at the mercy of the dragoons. Their churches were destroyed. Soldiers could be billeted in their homes and make free with anything – and anyone – they found in them. Unless their officers put restrictions on them, no one else dared to do so. Tens of thousands of Huguenots had already fled the country, and more of them were on the move, while those who remained were under constant pressure to be converted to the Roman Catholic faith. Only so could their civil rights be assured. Anyone suspected of having Protestant sympathies was liable to be branded as a heretic, and there was tension in all the religious groups that were not strictly orthodox. The Quietists, similar in many ways to the Puritans in England, were in particular viewed with suspicion. Although Madame Guyon had never joined them, her views, and her emphasis on the development of the inner life of the soul, were in many ways similar to theirs, and she was considered to be one of them.

The political climate in France was electric, too. With Protestant Europe up in arms at the treatment being meted out to the Huguenots, Louis was all the more eager to maintain good relations with Rome, though determined to assert the right of the Gallican Church as outlined in 'The Declaration of the Clergy of France' in 1682. In such an atmosphere it was not difficult for astute persons to bring about the downfall of those against whom they had a grudge, as Madame Guyon and Father La Combe were soon to find.

Even as they travelled towards Paris their spirits were oppressed by a sense of impending tragedy.

'All along the road something within said to me the same words as St. Paul: "I go up to Jerusalem and the Spirit tells me everywhere that crosses and chains await me." I could not prevent myself expressing it to my most familar friends, who used their efforts to stop me on the road,' Madame Guyon reported.

'What do you want to go there for?' she was asked in Grenoble, where she had gone to collect her daughter and the maid. 'To be crucified? Don't go to Paris! Don't go!' But go on she must, impelled by the same inner conviction as sent the apostle Paul to Jerusalem.

With Father La Combe it was the same. 'Would it not be a fine thing, and very glorious to God, if he desired to make us in that great city serve as a spectacle to men and angels!' he said. Theirs was the true spirit of martyrdom.

Actually, things went very well for La Combe at first. He was given important preaching assignments, and his eloquence and evident sincerity had people flocking to hear him. His star was in the ascendant, and had it not been for Father de la Mothe it might well have continued so.

Father de la Mothe, however, had different plans for his junior colleague, whose success as a preacher stirred his jealousy, and whose close friendship with his half-sister stirred his avarice. She still had an income on which he would have liked to lay hands, and Father La Combe, as her spiritual director, could have instructed her to hand it over. This he had refused to do. Furthermore, he was handling a financial matter for her of which Father de la Mothe disapproved. It had to do with the girl Madame Guyon had saved from sexual involvement with the little Bishop in Gex. She felt herself responsible for the girl, as it was due to her influence that she had now left the new Catholic convent in Gex and was seeking admittance into another Order. Madame Guyon knew the value of a dowry in such circumstances. 'As she is beautiful, although extremely discreet, there is always ground for fear when one is exposed without a fixed settlement.' So she had deposited a sum of money for that purpose with Father La Combe, and Father de la Mothe let him know that if he did not persuade Madame Guyon to give it instead for a wall he himself wanted built in his own monastery, there would be trouble.

'But Father La Combe, always upright, said that he could not conscientiously advise me to do anything else than what he knew I had resolved to do in favour of the girl.'

On such a trivial matter (the sum of money was not great) Father La Combe's fate was apparently sealed. Father de la Mothe, already prejudiced against him, got to work to bring about his downfall.

Father La Combe, he told his fellow Barnabites, was a disgrace to their Order. It was a scandal that he had actually stayed in inns with Madame Guyon on their journey to Paris, instead of going to spend the night at the Barnabite monasteries en route. (He did not mention that there were no Barnabite monasteries en route). Furthermore, Father La Combe was a Savoyard, and the yoke of the Savoyards in their Order should be shaken off. It was an insult to the French nation that every six years a Savoyard should be made Provincial of the Barnabites, he said.

Then rumours were circulated that Father La Combe's theology was wrong, that he was connected with the Spanish priest Molinos, the leader of the Quietists, who had just been tried and found guilty of heresy, and charged with immorality into the bargain.

Father La Combe's theology had already been passed as correct when he was called to Rome, and he had Attestations to that effect, which would have exonerated him from the charge of heresy. The suave Father de la Mothe, on the pretext that he wanted to show them to the Archbishop of Paris, and thereby prove La Combe's orthodoxy, obtained possession of the precious documents. They were never seen again.

The next step was to make representations to the King

himself. Father La Combe was suspected of heresy. A *lettre de cachet* was issued ordering Father La Combe not to go outside the Barnabite House until he had been questioned by the ecclesiastical chancellor. But Father de la Mothe saw to it that Father La Combe was not told of the royal order. He therefore went about his duties in the usual way, and when news reached him that one of his penitents had been knocked down by a cart, he went, as requested, to her to receive her confession.

That was sufficient. His absence was reported. He had disobeyed the King's order! He was arrested, and sent to the Bastille.

Although he had known nothing about the *lettre de cachet* and its orders, he was not taken by surprise. For weeks he had been conscious of Father de la Mothe's suppressed antagonism, and knew what it might lead to. 'The weather is very lowering,' he wrote significantly in a letter to Madame Guyon during that period. 'I do not know when the thunderbolts will fall, but all will be welcome from the hand of God.' and one day, when she went as usual to his confessional, he managed to tell her that he found himself longing for the 'disgrace and ignominy' that he sensed awaited him.

'I am going to say the Mass,' he said. 'Listen to it – and sacrifice me to God, as I myself am going to sacrifice myself to Him.' It was his conscious act of submission to the will of God.

The solemnity of those quiet moments in the confessional box, when the monk from the hills of Savoy murmured the familiar words of the Mass, and the woman whose spirit was knit to his knelt with her head bowed, must have been not unlike that which reigned in Gethsemane.

They never met again. Five days later came his arrest, and she knew her own hour would soon come.

It came after a period of tension and humiliation, mainly caused by Father de la Mothe. Pretending concern for her, he told her she also was under suspicion and urged her to flee from Paris, back to Montargis. This she refused to do, saying that flight would be tantamount to acknowledging her guilt, and would further implicate Father La Combe. Then he tried to incite the Archbishop of Paris against her, but she was so ably and loyally defended by the guardian of her children, a Councillor of Parliament, that that attempt to incriminate her failed too.

Meanwhile, rumours reflecting on her moral character were being spread abroad, and especially her connection with La Combe.

'Everyone cried out against me, except those who knew me personally, and knew how far removed I was from those things,' she wrote. 'But the others accused me of heresy, sacrilege, infamies of every kind, the nature of which I am even ignorant of, of hypocrisy, knavery. When I was at church I heard people behind me ridiculing me, and once I heard priests say that I ought to be thrown out of the church.' It was in circumstances like this that her spirit so often soared rather than sank. 'I cannot express how content I was inwardly, leaving myself entirely without reserve to God, quite ready to suffer the last penalty if such was His will.' But she had her periods of deep depression too, when she felt herself forsaken by God as well as by man, and despairingly abandoned herself to the eternal separation which she felt her sinful nature merited. Once again she fell ill, with headaches which nearly drove her crazy, and a violent cough.

Meanwhile Father de la Mothe, having failed to get her in his power by becoming her spiritual director (she stead-fastedly refused to accept him in this capacity) devised a plan whereby she should be put in detention. The King was informed that she was a heretic, that she had constant correspondence with Molinos – 'I, who did not know there was such a person as Molinos in the world until I learned it in the *Gazette*!' – that she had written a dangerous book and to cap it all, that she held secret assemblies. All her teaching on prayer and the cultivation of the inner life had been done on a one to one basis, but from Father de la Mothe's point of view, they were secret assemblies. On the shaky foundation of this last accusation a great many people she had never seen or even heard about were exiled, including one man whose sole crime was having been heard to remark that her little book on prayer was very good.

The holding of secret assemblies constituted a threat to public security in the tense atmosphere of those days. To reinforce this particular accusation a letter purporting to have been written by her was forged, in which she said she had great designs, but that the arrest of Father La Combe had endangered them, that she no longer held assemblies in her own house, as she was too closely watched, but that she would hold them elsewhere.

'It was on this fictitious letter, which was shown to His Majesty, that the order to imprison me was given.' On the Eve of St. Francis de Sales, in January 1688, she was sent to a convent in a suburb of Paris, where she was shut up alone in a small room with only a hard-faced nun to bring her meals and report on what she did. The worst of it, from her point of view, was the complete separation from her daughter, with whom no correspondence was to be allowed, and of whom no news would reach her. In this state of isolation she was kept until the time of her first interrogation.

*   *   *

Madame Guyon usually acquitted herself very well when she was brought before interrogators and judges. The latent ability which had revealed itself when, as a young married woman, she had dealt successfully with the demand from Monsieur for the payment of a debt she had never incurred, when as a widow she had straightened out her husband's tangled affairs, was brought into play when she had to defend her faith and her activities. The only times when she failed were when, through anxiety to do and say the right things, she became taut and watchful of her own reactions. She blamed herself for this, and learned to commit herself, her words and her reactions to God as she went to answer the questions that would be fired at her. Time and time again she was to prove the reliability of the promise Christ made to his disciples when he warned them they would be arrested and brought to trial, and then said, 'Settle it therefore in your minds not to meditate beforehand how to answer, for I will give you a mouth and wisdom which none of your adversaries will be able to withstand or contradict.'

She was in a good position to stand on that assurance, for she had nothing to hide, and a carelessness of what happened to her freed her from tension. She went to the first interrogation calmly, to face a Doctor of the Sorbonne and an official. Polite preliminaries over, they started their questioning.

Her association with Father La Combe was the first subject to be raised.

'Did not Father La Combe take you with him from France to Savoy?'

'No. He could not possibly have accompanied me when I went to Savoy. He had not been in France for ten years when I went there.'

'But he has taught you the practice of prayer, has he not?'

'It is not Father La Combe who has taught me to pray. I have practised prayer from my youth, long before I knew him. Actually, I never even met him until he came to my husband's home bringing a letter to me from my half-brother, Father de la Mothe. I did not see him again for ten years, when I left France and went to Savoy.'

The Doctor of the Sorbonne, who was merely performing his official duty in interrogating her, put an end to that part of the discussion. There was no point in pursuing it when the facts could be so easily verified.

'There is no ground here for a serious enquiry,' he said firmly. 'Let us pass on to the next question. Madame, this book entitled *Short and Easy Method of Prayer* written under your name. Is it not true that Father La Combe really wrote it?'

'No, he did not. I wrote it myself. He was not even in the neighbourhood when I wrote it. He was in Verceil, in Italy.

I was in Grenoble in France. I had no thought of its being published,' she continued. 'That happened when a friend of mine, a Counsellor of Grenoble, saw the manuscript on my table one day when he came to visit me, and asked if he might read it. As he found it helpful, he asked me to allow it to be printed. He asked me to write a preface and divide it into chapters, which I did one afternoon. Father La Combe had nothing to do with it.'

Father La Combe's name was dropped from the interrogations after that. The contents of the book itself would now be examined, she was told.

Her reaction was prompt and disarming. She was glad that it should be examined. She had never intentionally departed from the faith of the Holy Church, she declared. She would, indeed, give her life for it. She had already submitted the little book to the theologians, and was prepared to do so again. She had had no theological training, and could readily understand if some of the expressions she had used needed correction. All she had wanted to do was to help people who did not know how to pray.

'But do you not want to do away with the vocal prayers said in church?' her interrogators asked, and pointed to a place in which she had advocated the quiet, slow recital of the Lord's Prayer in private as being worth more than repeating it automatically many times aloud.

'But to teach a prayer with attention and application to one's own condition is not to do away with prayer. On the contrary, it establishes prayer, and makes it sincere.'

The Doctor of the Sorbonne nodded. He had no fault to find with that. 'If you had explained yourself like this in the book itself, you would not be here,' he said, after raising several other points, all of which she answered to his satisfaction.

'But the explanations *are* there,' she protested. 'You will find them at the end of each chapter. If there is anything wrong with them, you should not hold me responsible, but the doctors who approved and passed them!'

She had won another round, and the interrogations took

another line. The men arrived for the fourth time, this time with a letter which the official read aloud to her. It was the forged letter, of which she knew nothing until she listened to what she was supposed to have written to a Father Francis, of whom she had never heard.

'My Father, do not come to see me at the Cloister of Notre Dame. I am being watched, and can no longer hold assemblies at the usual place.' The letter went on to refer to plans against the State, and ended with the significant words, 'I do not sign because of the evil times.'

'There!' said the official with an air of finality. 'You can see, Madame, that after a letter like this there was good reason to put you in prison.'

'Yes, sir,' she answered. Then she added drily, 'If I had written it!'

'But you did write it.'

'No, I did not. Anyone who knows me would tell you it is not in my style, nor in my handwriting. It is a forgery.'

'Then we must find out who the forger is!' said the official contemptuously.

'It is the scribe Gautier,' replied Madame Guyon. She had heard about that man's secret profession from his own wife, and from the official's start of surprise she perceived that she had hit the nail on the head. She perceived something else, too. The guilty way in which he folded up the letter and said they would say no more about it convinced her that what she had already suspected was a fact. But the official was in league with Father de la Mothe, and with the affair in his hands there was little hope that she would be exonerated. The Doctor of the Sorbonne, his duty in taking part in the interrogations fulfilled, put in a good word for her, but it had no effect. She remained imprisoned in the convent, and occupied her time in writing poetry, letters to friends, and what was to prove of even greater interest to posterity, her autobiography.

The thought of La Combe was persistent as she wrote it. He had urged her years ago to do it, and she had been reluctant to obey at the time. Now it seemed to be the one practical

thing she could do to demonstrate her submission to him as
her spiritual director, and also to vindicate him by relating
the truth about their association. From the confinement of
the little convent cell where she spent months alone, came
the strange medley of incidents and experiences, dreams and
visions, homilies and prayers which were to bewilder and
mystify, challenge and inspire her readers for centuries to
come. While others were busying themselves with her affairs
outside, she was producing something which would go on
speaking long after the strident voices of her enemies had
been silenced and forgotten.

When the official interrogations were over her long periods
of solitary confinement were interspersed with interviews of
another character. She had feared for her daughter, and
when writing to one friend ended her letter with the touching
words, 'When I came here my daughter was taken from me.
Those who took her from me do not allow me to know where
she is. You will permit me, if you can obtain a knowledge of
her situation, to ask your friendly interest on her behalf.' Her
fears were not without foundation, for she was approached
with suggestions that she should consent to the girl being
married to a nephew of the Archbishop of Paris. If she would
agree to the marriage, she was told, she would be set free
within a week.

Madame Guyon knew enough about the man proposed as
her son-in-law to refuse the suggestion out of hand.

'I said I would not purchase my liberty at the price of
sacrificing my daughter; that I was content to remain in
prison as long as it should please our Lord.' They tried more
than once to wrest her consent from her, but she adamantly
resisted. On other occasions she was urged to write a
confession that she had been wrong in some of her views, and
that she had been unduly influenced in them by Father La
Combe.

'I would rather die than tell such a falsehood!' was her
reply. She had heard that Father La Combe had been very
kindly treated in the Bastille, and that when he had been

transferred elsewhere the commandant in charge of him had recognised his godliness.

'Consequently the commandant, full of love for the truth, wrote that this Father was a man of God, and that he begged some alleviation of his imprisonment might be granted.' That letter reached the Archbishop of Paris, who showed it to Father de la Mothe – and La Combe was taken off to a desert isle, out of reach of the commandant who favoured him. 'O God, nothing is concealed from you. Will you for long leave your servant in ignominy and grief?' she wrote feelingly. The last thing she was likely to do was betray the trust of one with whom she was so one in spirit as La Combe. On the face of it, his lot was harder than hers. Although she sometimes felt that all her friends had deserted her, and that she would be incarcerated in the convent for life, she had evidence from time to time that there were those in influential positions who were loyal to her, and working for her release. La Combe had no such assurance. The Barnabite from Savoy had no friends in court in Paris, and the evidence that should have told in his favour, those Attestations from Rome, had been suppressed. For him was reserved the honour accorded to those referred to in the book of Hebrews, as being those of whom the world was not worthy. As Madame Guyon wrote, 'only eternity will show who have been the true friends of God.'

Meanwhile, a series of events in no way related to her was taking place in the court of France itself, which were to lead to her deliverance from an entirely unexpected quarter. Madame de Maintenon, by now the morganatic wife of King Louis XIV, and the most powerful woman in the kingdom, took up the cudgels on her behalf. This is how it came about.

Madame de Maintenon, having made a moral man of the King, and setting the example of piety in a court that had been renowned for its corruption, took little interest in its social activities, and showed herself there but seldom. She provided the King with a comfortable domestic life, and when he was not performing his kingly duties he was usually to be found in her apartment, whence he retreated, like any other happily married man, when it was time to go home. Her own personal preoccupation, however, was not to be found in the palace of Versailles, which held out little attraction for her. The darling project of her heart was in the establishment of what amounted to a sort of boarding school for girls of noble birth whose fathers were in what might be termed reduced circumstances. At St. Cyr they would receive a good education and practise a devout life. It was something new, and she was responsible for bringing it into being. She appointed the staff, was consulted on all matters concerning it, and took a personal interest in the pupils.

One of them was a pretty little girl who was likely to be rather homesick, so Madame de Maintenon suggested that her older sister, a canoness, should join the staff in order to be near the child. Now it so happened that the canoness was a first cousin of Madame Guyon's, knew of the injustice of her imprisonment, and seized an opportunity to speak to Madame de Maintenon about her. Nothing came of it at the time, but her name was introduced.

Then Madame de Maintenon heard it again, this time from a personal friend who had gone to visit the prioress of the very convent where Madame Guyon was imprisoned, and came back with a surprisingly good report of her. The prioress and her nuns, who had been filled with righteous indignation at what they had heard of the heresies and the immoral behaviour of their prisoner, had all changed their minds. They could not speak highly enough of her piety, her sincerity, her humility, her love for God. They simply did not believe the tales that had been told about her.

Finally, a relative of Madame de Maintenon herself, an abbess, had come to Paris on business matters, one of which concerned the young nun from the New Catholics in Gex. The abbess was very annoyed with the Archbishop of Paris, and said so. The girl was to enter her Order, Madame Guyon was prepared to pay her dowry, but Madame Guyon was imprisoned in a convent, and the abbess could not get at her.

The Archbishop of Paris refused to allow anyone to see her. 'It is a business of charity Madame Guyon is doing in favour of a poor girl, whom I want to make a nun in my House, and the Archbishop is hindering it. I can't get that dowry. It is very unjust,' said the abbess.

This got things moving at last. Madame de Maintenon compiled the facts of the case, then brought them before the king. The accusations brought against this woman had never been proved, and yet she was still being held a prisoner. The king shrugged his shoulders, and ordered the Archbishop to set her at liberty. The Archbishop hummed and hawed a bit, saying certain formalities must be observed first, but though he managed to delay things for a few days, he had to yield to the command of His Majesty. When the day came for her release, the guardian of her children came to take her to the home of Madame de Maintenon's personal friend, where she was re-united with her family. To crown it all, a thoroughly suitable marriage was arranged for her daughter. She was betrothed to the Count of Vaux, a relative of her old friend, the Duchess of Charost.

The tide had turned for Madame Guyon, and she would not have been human if she had not been thankful for it. All the same, her friends and well-wishers exhibited greater relief and excitement than she herself, and in her auto-biography she wrote a strangely revealing little sentence, 'I had more perceptible joy on entering my prison than on leaving it.' Inner peace and joy, she had proved, are not dependent on circumstances. But there was something about the whole affair which kindled her amazement as she looked back to those early days in Gex, remembering her anxiety over the young nun, and then the steps she took on her behalf to ensure her security.

'I marvelled, O my God, at Your divine providence, and the special evidences of Your control. This same money, which has been the first source of all my troubles, through Father de la Mothe's desire to have it, You have made, O my God, the means of my liberty!'

I think we should be careful, in stating the doctrine of faith, not to place it in opposition to reason. On the contrary, we only say what is sustained both by St. Paul and St. Augustine, when we assert that it is a very reasonable thing to believe. Faith is different from mere physical and emotive impulse; and it would be no small mistake to confound those who walk by faith, with thoughtless and impulsive persons and enthusiasts.

Faith is necessarily based upon antecedent acts of intelligence. By the use of these powers of perception and reasoning, which God has given us, we have the knowledge of the existence of God. It is by their use, also, that we know that God has spoken to us in His revealed word . . . And it is our duty, in the exercise of faith in the goodness and wisdom of Him who issues the command, to yield obedience, and to go wherever it may lead us, however dark and mysterious the path may now appear.

Francis S. Fenelon, Paris, August 11th, 1689,
in a letter written to Madame Guyon

9

Enter Fenelon

The Abbé de Fenelon, tall, courteous, immaculately dressed, every inch an aristocrat, was on his way to Paris from Poitou, whither he had been sent to convert the Protestants in the neighbourhood to the Roman Catholic faith. He had gone willingly enough, but on one condition – that the militia were to be withdrawn. He would have in his area no dragoons invading Huguenot homes, roasting the men before the fire, rifling their coffers, raping the women-folk, all in the name of religion. The gentle Abbé was horrified at such tactics, and would have none of them. If people could not be convinced inwardly, their conversion would be utterly false and worth nothing. He had set about convincing them by his quietly persuasive arguments, his eloquent preaching; more than anything, perhaps, by his own unselfconscious goodness. If his task had been made the easier by the undeniable fact that converts to the faith would regain the civil rights they had lost with the revocation of the Edict of Nantes, that was through no conniving on his part. Nor did he hold it out as a reason for accepting the primacy of the Pope along with the Holy Scriptures. His success in Poitou was due to no outward violence or inward subversion, and the ecclesiastical world in France and beyond knew it, and approved. The Abbé de Fenelon was recognised as an up and coming ecclesiastic in that year of grace, 1688, destined for a high position in the Catholic hierarchy.

If similar ideas concerning his career had presented themselves to him, he would have thrust them from him in shame. His aim was to follow His Master, share His ignominy, suffer with Him, not to gain earthly promotion, even in the Church. The mystical streak in his nature drew him towards the fathomless depths and heights of a spiritual relationship of oneness with the eternal. This was the goal towards which he strove, and he refused to be diverted towards anything else. He was familiar with the writings of the mystics, St. John of the Cross and St. Francis de Sales among them. But he was on his guard against the heresies that could so easily insinuate themselves into the teachings of the uninstructed and viewed with reservation the Quietists, whose leader, Molinos, was still in the news, on trial before the Inquisition. For this reason his interest in a woman of whom he had heard, a Madame Guyon who was reputedly secretly one of them, and whose influence on many of the people he knew had surprised him, was tempered with a fear lest both her theology and her moral character were faulty.

As his way back to Paris led through her home town, Montargis, he made some discreet enquiries about her, and found her reputation there was beyond reproach. She was known to be very devout, extremely generous to the poor, and her gentleness and patience under great provocation had gained for her the name of a saint. He went on to Paris with his interest in her quickened, though he was cautious enough to keep quiet about it when he met his fellow-clerics, especially those like Bossuet whom he had loved and admired from his youth. Bossuet, he had reason to know, had little sympathy with the Quietists. In fact, he realised that he was more likely to hear about her from members of the laity, like the Dukes of Beauvilliers and Chevreuse, or the Duchess of Charost, all friends of his.

Eventually it was through the Duchess that he first met her personally. The Duchess invited him to her home to meet Madame Guyon, an old friend of hers, with whom she believed he would find he had much in common. And so came about a meeting which was to fall into the category known as historic, when a woman suspected of heresy met a scion of the established Catholic Church of Rome, and they found themselves to be one.

Not that it happened immediately. When the aristocratic Fenelon, his inherent reserve clothed in the cultured urbanity of the age, first met the demurely dressed widow of whom he had heard, he did not take to her, and she realised it. 'I felt within me that this first interview did not satisfy him,' she wrote in her autobiography, and she was sorry about it. She had had one of her intuitive flashes about him, and had expected an immediate affinity, a recognition of spiritual unity. 'He did not relish me.' However, she met him again the next day, and this time as they talked together he understood her better. As they were both to return to Paris that evening (he was Superior of the New Catholic Establishment near to where she lived), they travelled in the same carriage, her maid accompanying them. During that quiet journey he learned enough about her to realise that she was not the neurotic religious charlatan that some had represented her as being, but the genuine article, a woman of God, with a depth of spiritual experience and perception that matched, perhaps even surpassed, his own.

This was her opportunity to disclose what was in her heart, to talk to one whom she felt instinctively to be a kindred spirit, to share and compare experiences in prayer, and the knowledge of God. She believed all could pray, have direct access to God, she said. 'All who are willing to pray can easily do it with the assistance of the Holy Spirit, Who is given to all Christians.' She knew this from her own experience, and that there is a swift, silent, inward prayer that can be made at all times, without distracting from the business on hand. 'It is not the prayer of the head, but the prayer of the heart.'

For what did she ask when she prayed? From her point of

view, prayer was not so much to receive anything from God as to please Him, place herself at His disposal, do His will. Fenelon agreed. But she taught others to pray – how did she do this?

'I tell them that one way to place themselves in His presence is by meditation. Meditation by reading. I tell them to take some mighty truth which provides food for thought, and also for practice. I warn them not to rush from truth to truth, but to ponder on one – to read just a little, say two or three lines, then stop and think about it. Bees cannot draw out the juice of flowers by flying over them. They must settle and suck if they are to draw out the nourishment. So with us.'

Faith was essential, too. They must believe that God had come to dwell within them. Jesus Christ Himself had said that if any man loved Him and kept His commandments, He and His Father would come and make their abode with him. But for God to have complete control there – ah, that was something deeper. Conversion was not complete as long as it only turned from sin to grace. Rectifying outward bad habits and behaviour was an indispensable step, but it was only the first one. The inner life must be purified, too, and only God could do that. 'He had a drawing power which attracts the soul always more and more strongly to Himself, and in drawing it He purifies it.'

God purifies it? Then what about the value of self-imposed mortification and austerities?

God's salvation is given, not earned, she declared. All virtue which is not given from within is only a mask, like a garment, merely covering what is really there. Man-made virtue becomes self-righteousness. Take the Lord's parable of the publican and the Pharisee. 'The publican seeing in himself only sinfulness, hates himself. The Pharisee, on the other hand, supported by the great number of works of righteousness he feels he has performed, seems to hold his salvation in his own hands, and regards heaven as the recompense due to his merits. . . God apparently preferred the sinner!'

'All true virtue comes hand in hand with the possession of God.' The knowledge of God, union with God, – Fenelon realised that this was what absorbed her, this was the goal to which she had been urged. And the greatest obstacle in achieving it, she declared, was the subtle, tenacious enemy within – SELF. It had to die.

'Whatever is of man, and of his own doing, must die. However noble and exalted it be, it must die. All our self-sufficiency must be destroyed. And God alone can do it. We can never do it ourselves. We love our ego, our SELF, too much. We don't want it to be destroyed! If God did not do it Himself, we would never consent to it.'

But that brought up the matter of the freedom of the will. Has not God given to man free will, the right to choose?

'Yes, indeed. I cannot endure people saying we are not free to resist grace. We *are* free to resist grace.'

Then this destruction of SELF, to which we cannot consent, how explain God's action in doing it, if it is contrary to our own will? Where is the freedom of the will?

Madame Guyon had a very simple answer to that.

'The freedom of the will implies the right to surrender it. A person who has given himself to God at the beginning of his Christian course, has given an active consent to whatever God should do.'

Again, she could speak from experience, and made no effort to disguise what had been involved. There had never been any doubt but that it would include suffering. Had not Jesus Christ clearly said that those who would be His disciples must be prepared to deny themselves, take up the cross and follow Him? But what form the cross would take was not usually divulged. God warned that it would be painful, without specifying what form the suffering would take. 'If we knew and understood beforehand, we would shrink back. But God only asks of us our free will. It is the only thing we have that we can sacrifice to Him. So we surrender our own will that He may make of us what He pleases – for time and for eternity.'

Fenelon had nothing to quarrel with in that. It was no new theology. Jesus Christ Himself had said, 'Not as I will, but as Thou wilt.' The surrender of the will was a voluntary act. Only through death could the new life come. The seed must die to bring fruit. But life, abundant life, truly followed death, and fruit was brought from the seed that died. No one seeing and listening to her could have doubted that.

But what about those seasons of spiritual dryness, which all the saints seemed to have experienced? Sometimes God hides Himself, she said, to rouse us from our lethargy and laziness, and make us seek Him earnestly. But there is something else. There is a pathway to be trodden from relying on feelings of peace and joy and zeal, to naked faith.

Naked faith. It was a phrase she often used. Faith that is not dependent on feelings.

'It is very important to prevent people from dwelling on visions and ecstasies, because this arrests them all their life.' She had had her share of visions and ecstasies, but they had not prevented that long, long period of spiritual darkness while still in Montargis. 'Besides,' she continued, 'these graces are very subject to illusions, for what has form, image and distinctness, together with the delight of the senses, can very well be imitated by the devil. . .'

One can only speculate on the subjects that were touched on in that quiet drive to Paris, during which the gracious, intelligent Fenelon found himself completely at one with the widow who, if she expressed herself rather incoherently, quite obviously knew what she was talking about. It was the beginning of a life-long fellowship which stood the test of acute trials, particularly in the case of Fenelon, whose loyalty to her cost him very dear.

The relationship was completely free of the sexual element without which the twentieth century finds it almost impossible to recognise a spiritual unity between a man and a woman, although it is in line with mystics of the past – St. Francis of Assisi and Clare, St. John of the Cross and Teresa of Avila, St. Francis de Sales and Madame Chantal. However, the wildest imaginations of rumour-mongers could find no grounds on which to suggest that there was anything of that sort between Madame Guyon and Fenelon. But of the spiritual affinity there can be no doubt. As Madame Guyon wrote, in her usual ardent style, 'It seems to me that my soul has perfect rapport with his, and those words of David regarding Jonathan, that "his soul cleaved to that of David" appeared to me suitable for this union.'

During the two years following that conversation, a voluminous correspondence was maintained between them (over one hundred letters from Madame Guyon, thirty-odd from Fenelon) and occasional meetings in the homes of mutual friends. One of those was the Duke of Beauvilliers. When he was appointed as Governor of the household of the Dauphin's eldest son, second heir to the throne, he immediately appointed Fenelon as the child's tutor. The little Duc de Bourgogne was known to have an abominable temper, so Fenelon would have his work cut out to mould him into a wise and self-controlled prince, one who would be fit to mount the throne of Europe's greatest kingdom. But Madame Guyon had no doubt about his ability to do so – so far, that is, as he acted in complete dependence on God, and by dying to himself, as she did not fail to remind him. As for his royal pupil, she was convinced that God would make a saint of him. The gradual transformation of the boy's character during his years under Fenelon's tutelage proved her to be correct.

As for Madame Guyon herself, she had reached the peak, humanly speaking, of her varied and dramatic career. She was now the intimate friend of some of the noblest in the land, including the powerful Madame de Maintenon herself, who invited her to visit St. Cyr and instruct the young ladies there in the path of simple faith and prayer, and the acceptance of the will of God in their personal lives. Her days were often filled, as in Grenoble, with private interviews, and she maintained a wide correspondence with the individuals she had been brought in touch with over the course of the years.

One of these was Father La Combe. She devised means of communicating with him by letter from time to time, and on one occasion wrote advising him to employ his time in imprisonment in the way she herself had done when confined to the convent. Writing had been her outlet then – her autobiography, her poems, and letters to friends. Writing had, in fact, always been an outlet for her, a means of giving expression to her thoughts and aspirations, her feelings and the spiritual revelations that had been given to her. Now he was shut off from the active ministry that had filled his life previously, might not his letters from prison, like those of St. Paul, eventually have an even wider influence on generations to come?

But Father La Combe was not made that way.

'Alas!' he wrote in reply. 'Can the dry rock send forth flowing fountains? I never had much power or inclination for such efforts; and this seclusion from the world, this imprisonment, these cold and insensible walls, seem to have taken from me the power which I once had. The head, not the heart, seems to have become withered and hard, like rock. Like the Jews of old. I sit down by the waters of my place of exile and hang my harp upon the willows.

'It is true there has been some mitigation of my state. I am now permitted to go beyond the walls of my prison into the neighbouring gardens and fields, but it is only on the condition of my labouring there without cessation from morning till evening. What then can I do? How can I meditate? What can I think? – except upon the manner of subduing earth and of cultivating plants. I will add, however, that I have no choice for myself. All my desires are summed up in one – that God may be glorified in me.'

Prisons Do Not Exclude God

Strong are the walls around me
   That hold me all the day;
But they who thus have bound me
   Cannot keep God away;
My very dungeon walls are dear
Because the God I love is here.

They know, who thus oppress me,
   'Tis hard to be alone;
But know not, One can bless me
   Who comes through bars and stone
He makes my dungeon's darkness bright
And fills my bosom with delight

Thy love, O God, restores me
   From sighs and tears to praise;
And deep my soul adores Thee
   Nor thinks of time or place.
I ask no more, in good or ill,
But union with Thy holy will.

Jeanne de la Mothe Guyon

10

Pilloried

Outwardly things appeared to be going very well for Madame Guyon. She was accepted as a spiritual leader by some of the highest in the land, including Madame de Maintenon herself; her books were circulating widely, her daughter had married a most suitable man, her younger son had gained a commission in the army. Although she was rarely free from the nervous disorder or physical pain that dogged her (the smallpox had left her with an eye that frequently became agonizingly inflamed) she managed to get through an incredible amount of writing, in addition to the many interviews and talks she gave at St. Cyr.

This period, however, was darkened by a continual fog of rumours about her, and suggestions that she was secretly disseminating the teaching of the heretic, Molinos.

'When I was in the country staying with my daughter, they said I instructed the peasants, though I saw none of them. If I was in the town, according to their story, they made me receive persons, or else I went to see them; and yet I neither saw them or knew them.' She longed to get away from it all. The desire that had been born in her when a child revived – the desire to retire into the seclusion of a convent, to live out her earthly existence quietly in prayer, meditation, worship, free from the publicity and the harassments that beset her everywhere she went. At one stage she got in touch with the prioress of the Benedictine Convent in Montargis, and arrangements were even being made for her to slip away there secretly, to be virtually incarcerated in a little cell for the rest of her life. She went so far as having the small amount of furniture necessary sent on ahead, when news got out of what was happening, and a stop was put to it.

'My friends and my enemies, if so one may call persons to whom one wishes no ill, opposed my project from different views; the former, not to lose me altogether; and the latter, in order to ruin me, and not allow their prey to escape. They considered that such a life as I wished to lead would give the lie to all the calumnies they had hitherto invented, and take from them all means of persecuting me more. I saw myself, then, obliged by both, who prayed the Archbishop to forbid my being received, to live in the world, in spite of my aversion to the world.'

Then, after three years of being in favour with Madame de Maintenon, she sensed a subtle change in that lady's attitude towards her. What lay behind it was not entirely clear. It may have been Madame de Maintenon's fear that the King would be angry with her for so close an association with the Quietist movement, of which he was becoming increasingly suspicious. It may have been her jealousy of the unique relationship between Madame Guyon and the Abbé de Fenelon. Madame de Maintenon tended to see herself as the spiritual mother of a renewed and pious court, yet here was Fenelon, the most heavenly-minded ecclesiastic in Paris, intimate friend of the devout and aristocratic Beauvilliers group, acknowledging the pockmarked widow, not herself, as the one from whom he derived the greatest spiritual inspiration. Indeed, on one occasion, he had written to her, Madame de Maintenon, frankly pointing out that her ego, her SELF, was still her unbroken idol. That she wanted to love God with all her heart, but not through the death of that SELF. That if she would yield herself wholly to the Spirit of God, to have all the roots of her egoism cut away, her faults would gradually disappear. Madame de Maintenon took it very well at the time, but assuming Fenelon's assessment to be accurate, it is not likely to have predisposed her towards the woman whose ego he deemed to have been completely dealt with.

If secret, unacknowledged jealousy was at the root of the change of manner of France's most powerful woman towards her, Madame Guyon allowed no such suspicion to creep into her autobiography. She wrote with uncharacteristic brevity of the tranquil period when she enjoyed her favour, summing it up in one paragraph:

'Since my release I had continued to go to St. Cyr, and some of the girls of that House having declared to Madame de Maintenon that in the conversations I had with them they found something which led them to God, she permitted them to put confidence in me; and on many occasions she testified, owing to the change in some with whom hitherto she had not been satisfied, that she had no cause for repenting it. She then showed me much kindness and, during three of four years that this lasted, I received from her every mark of esteem and confidence. But it is this very thing in the sequel which has drawn down upon me the greatest persecution. The *entrée* Madame de Maintenon gave me at St. Cyr, and the confidence shown me by some young ladies of the court, distinguished by their rank and by their piety, began to cause uneasiness to the persons who had persecuted me. They stirred up the directors to take offence, and under the pretence of the troubles I had had some years before, and of the great progress, as they said, of Quietism, they engaged the Superior of St. Cyr to represent to Madame de Maintenon that I disturbed the order of her House by a private direction; and that the girls whom I saw were so strongly attached to what I said to them, that they no longer listened to their Superior. Madame de Maintenon caused me to be told in a kindly way. I ceased to go to St. Cyr. I no longer answered the girls who wrote to me, except by open letters, which passed through the hands of Madame de Maintenon.'

Her virtual expulsion from St. Cyr caused quite a stir. Once more her little book on prayer came under review. Having been almost compulsory reading in pious circles, it was now put discreetly out of sight except among the friends who remained loyal to her and her teaching – the influential Dukes of Beauvilliers and Chevreuse and their Duchesses with them. And the Abbé Fenelon.

Rumours about her multiplied. Questioners abounded. In order to escape from the publicity she disappeared from Paris for a while, living quietly in the country, then returned secretly to her little house in the capital. As far as she was concerned, she would have been thankful to subside into obscurity, and tried to do so. She told no one where she was living except Monsieur Fouquet, the uncle of her son-in-law, a man she could trust completely to look after her financial affairs and provide her with money as she needed it.

Her disappearance from public life only seemed to provide further opportunities for the spread of rumours, especially as it coincided with the arrival in Paris of a Sister Rose who asserted that she knew Madame Guyon to be a very wicked person who would do great harm to the Church. Sister Rose had appeared out of the blue, and as no one seemed to feel it necessary to enquire into her past, and as a good many people were quite prepared to believe what she said, the efforts of Madame Guyon's few influential friends to clear her reputation were unavailing. Sister Rose evidently had amazing powers of persuasion.

'This woman, about whom there was in fact something very extraordinary (she prided herself on knowing the most secret thoughts and having the most detailed knowledge, not only of things at a distance from her, but even of the future) persuaded Monsieur Boileau and persons of virtue and probity with whom he was in relation that the greatest service they could render to God was to decry me, and even to imprison me owing to the ills I was capable of causing.'

Subtle attacks were being made on her from other sources, too. A group of women known as the Daughters of Father Vautier went around various confessionals relating gross sins they had committed owing, they said, to following Madame Guyon's teaching. This infiltration, which cast reflections on her morals as well as her theology, eventually aroused the Dukes of Beauvilliers and Chevreuse to take action on her behalf. They and their wives knew her intimately, and were ready to stand by her. They prepared a memorandum outlining her life and activities which they intended presenting to King Louis himself. Coming from such a source, from aristocrats in high positions of responsibility, known for their integrity, it could scarcely have failed to have its effect, especially as Madame de Maintenon had agreed to be associated with it.

The fact that it never reached the King was entirely due to Madame Guyon herself. She wrote years later: 'I owe them the justice to make it known that it was no fault of theirs that the authority of the King was not employed to shield me from so much injustice. They drew up a memoir likely to influence him in my favour, giving him an account of the conduct I had observed, and was still observing in my retirement. Madame de Maintenon was to have supported it by her testimony.'

Then she added the significant words, 'But having had the kindness to communicate it to me, I believed God did not wish me to be justified by that channel, and I required of them that they should leave me to the rigours of His justice, whatever they might be. They consented to defer to my request. The memoir already presented was withdrawn, and they adopted the course of silence, which they have since continued, being no longer able to do anything in my favour, owing to the outburst and prejudice.'

And so she closed the door on what could have been her way of escape. Beyond the cryptic sentence 'I believed God did not wish me to be justified by that channel' she gave no indication of what may have been the reasons for her refusal. It is possible that she was already beginning to realise that something was going on which was aimed to bring about the downfall of people of far greater distinction than herself. In her secluded life she knew little of the wider issues that were at stake, or of the budding intrigue in which she would be little more than a cat's paw. Even with her prophetic intuitions she could not foresee that two of the leading prelates of France would be in open conflict over her teaching, and that the conflict would widen until it involved the King and the Pope. But she was wise enough to recognise that she, a widow from the provinces, was of insufficient importance to make it worthwhile to build up such a case against her, and that her little book on prayer would probably have been swept away unnoticed in the current flood of literature had it not received so much publicity in high quarters.

She had little doubt as to who would be embroiled. The friends who were planning to come out openly in her support were none other than those who had been entrusted with the upbringing of the second heir to the throne, the little Duc de Bourgogne. If her enemies succeeded in bringing her down, those who would suffer through having their names associated with hers were the Duke of Beauvilliers – and the Abbé Fenelon.

If this consideration is what weighed with her, bringing her to the point of refusing, in the name of God, the proffered help, it was one of the noblest decisions of her life. However, Madame Guyon rarely seemed to consider she had done anything worthy of mention. Giving away her fortune, renouncing her rights, founding little hospitals, setting poor people up in business – she passed them off in a few words, almost forgetting to mention them. It was a different matter when it came to what she suffered, although here again, the physical sufferings endured in difficult confinements, frequent eye inflammations and similar ills, were referred to as being of secondary consideration. The sufferings which she felt most acutely were the mental, emotional, and spiritual ones. These were the crosses to which she referred again and again in her autobiography. She accepted them (not always without a struggle) as from the hand of God for her own discipline and purification until she reached the stage when she no longer felt them as a personal affront, when the SELF within her no longer reacted in pride or anger or self-pity. She had learned, in the words of St. Paul, to reckon herself dead, as no longer existing, having no will apart from God's will. Fenelon, in one of his early letters to her, summarised her teaching better than she did herself, when he outlined the progressive stages in reaching that state.

1.   The first step taken by the soul that had deliberately given itself to God is to put right the things that are wrong in the life, and to correct evil habits. 'But it does not act alone; it follows and cooperates with the grace that is given it.'

2.   The next step is to stop depending on the feelings of joy and well-being that God often gives in the early experiences of spiritual life. 'When we lose our inward happiness, we are very apt to think that we lose God; not considering that the moral life of the soul does not consist in pleasure, but in union with God's will, whatever that may be.' We live by faith, not feelings.

3.   'Another step is the crucifixion of any reliance upon our virtues, either outward or inward . . . in our truth, temperance, faith, benevolence.' Dependence on one's personal virtues is one of the most subtle forms of SELF.

4.   The fourth step consists in ceasing to rebel against the reverses of life, but rather to receive them as from the hand of God, as necessary for the inward crucifixion of SELF. 'So clear is the soul's perception of God's presence in everything; so strong is its faith, that those apparently adverse dealings, once exceeding trying, are now received not merely with acquiescence, but with cheerfulness.'

5.   Now comes, as a fifth step, the new life, for when we have proceeded so far, the natural man is crucified, on the cross, and leads on to a life in union with God. 'It is then that there is such a harmony between the human and Divine will, that they may properly be regarded as having become one. This, I suppose, was the state of St. Paul, when he says, 'I live; yet not I, but Christ liveth in me.'

His summary did not stop there. He went on to speak of the will which is not merely passive under God's dealings, but what she called 'flexible', completely cooperative. And that the transformed soul continues to advance in holiness, with its capacity for love increasing. It was a long letter, and concluded as follows:

'Those who walk by faith walk in obscurity; but they know that there is a light above them, which will make all clear and bright in its appropriate time. We trust; but, as St. Paul says, we know in whom we have trusted.

'I illustrate the subject, Madame, in this way. I suppose myself to be in a strange country. There is a wide forest before me, with which I am totally unacquainted, although I must pass through it. I accordingly select a guide, whom I suppose to be able to conduct me through these ways never before trodden by me. In the following this guide, I obviously go by faith; but as I know the character of my guide, and as my intelligence or reason tells me that I ought to exercise such faith, it is clear that my faith in Him is not in opposition to reason, but is in accordance with it. On the contrary, if I refuse to have faith in my guide, and undertake to make my way through the forest by my own sagacity and reason, I may properly be described as a person without reason, or as unreasonable; and should probably suffer for my want of reason by losing my way. Faith and reason, therefore, if not identical, are not at variance.

'Fully subscribing, with these explanations, to the doctrine of faith as the life and guide of the soul, I remain, Madame, yours in our common Lord, Francis S. Fenelon.'

He had understood her perfectly, had expressed better than she could have expressed it herself, just what she believed.

She had found her way through these various stages, slowly and painfully, but now she had reached a point where the mental and spiritual sufferings had a new significance. They were as acute as ever, but they were borne for others rather than herself. There were souls for which she travailed, like St. Paul, until Christ was formed in them, until they could claim that the world was crucified to them, and they to the world. Although she undoubtedly led many to a first knowledge of Christ, her primary ministry was to those who already believed in Him.

'He made me understand that He did not call me, as had been thought, to a propagation of the external of the Church, which consists in winning heretics, but to the propagation of His Spirit, which is no other than the interior Spirit, and that it would be for this Spirit I would suffer. He does not even destine me for the first conversion of sinners, but to introduce those who are already touched with the desire of being converted into the perfect conversion, which is no other than this interior Spirit.'

There was also suffering of another type, as when she was confronted with evil in human form. One of these occasion was when Monsieur Fouquet brought to her a girl who admitted that she had sold herself to the devil in order to gain the affection of a valet of Monsieur Fouquet's. The poor valet, when he knew of it, went to his master in deep distress, and the girl was dismissed. However, Monsieur Fouquet was concerned for her welfare and brought her to Madame Guyon, believing that she could help her.

The moment she saw the girl, knowing nothing about her, Madame Guyon was conscious of an indescribable horror, and the girl was visibly alarmed as she faced her.

'This girl, while with me, often said, "You have something strong that I cannot endure." . . . I saw that God operated through me, without me, with His divine power. At last this power obliged her to tell me her frightful life, which makes me tremble as I think of it. She related to me the false pleasures that the Spirit of Darkness had procured for her; that he made her pass for a saint, perform visible austerities, but that he did not allow her to pray; that, as soon as she wished to do so, he appeared to her in a hideous form ready to devour her; that otherwise he appeared to her in a form as amiable as possible, and that he gave her all the money she wished.'

But he gave her no peace, the girl cried out in a terrible

voice, in reply to Madame Guyon's question, only hellish trouble.

'How different it is for me!' said Madame Guyon, and went on to assert that she had great inner happiness in serving Jesus Christ, even when she was ill and suffering incessant pain. 'And in order that you may know what that happiness is, I pray that you taste this peace of heart, if only for a moment.'

That prayer was answered with dramatic suddenness. The expression on the girl's face changed, and turning to Monsieur Fouquet, who was present, she exclaimed, 'Oh, sir! I feel so different. I was in hell, but now I'm in paradise!' Monsieur Fouquet promptly took her to the Grand Penitentiary in order that she might make her confession and promise amendment of life. The girl went on well for some months, but strange forces seemed to be abroad that were related to her. Two of those who were trying to help her were smitten unexpectedly with physical ills. The Grand Peninitentiary died suddenly. A Jacobin Father who had several times tried to save her from her depraved life also died. Then Madame Guyon was taken ill, and the girl came to see her.

'I knew you were very ill,' she said. 'The devil told me. He said he tried to kill you, but he was not permitted to. All the same, he said he would raise up so much trouble and persecution about you, that you'll die.'

The girl was being enmeshed again, lured back into the darkness. What was this about Satan having talked to her, having revealed his plans to her? Madame Guyon looked at her with dismay, realising that there was something different about her, and said sternly, 'You should not listen to the devil, not for a moment. Far less should you ever talk to him. I have told you that before. On no account enter into conversation with him. Tell him to go! Tell him you renounced him at your baptism, that you belong to Jesus Christ!'

But the damage had been done. The girl admitted that the

devil had persuaded her to go back on those vows of her baptism.

'Gone back on your vows!' Madame Guyon caught her breath, then urged the girl to renew the vows while there was yet time. 'It is not too late. Oh, give yourself anew to Jesus Christ! As for me, I don't mind what I have to suffer, if only you are truly converted.'

Her evident concern touched the girl, who said, 'You must love me very much to be willing to do so much for me.' But sinister spiritual forces had been unleashed that were too strong and subtle for her, and as though under a spell she went on, 'The devil told me he would do you so much harm, and stir up so many people against you, that you would die,' and as she spoke Madame Guyon again saw in imagination what she had seen years ago, in the New Catholic House in Gex – a bluish-coloured flame which turned into a hideous, horrifying face.

'But I had no fear of it, any more than of the threats he sent me. God for many years keeps me in the frame of mind that I would cheerfully give my life, even my peace which I value much more, for the salvation of a single soul.' And she meant it. But in the case of the girl who had sold herself to the devil, her efforts and willingness for sacrifice were in vain. One day a priest went to Monsieur Fouquet enquiring about her, and Monsieur Fouquet, unsuspecting, told him they had great hopes for her complete conversion, and at his request told him where she lived.

'When Monsieur Fouquet came to see me a little while after, and spoke to me of the priest, it occurred to me that it was that wicked priest of whom she had told me, with whom she had committed so many abominations. This proved only too true. She came no more.'

But Monsieur Fouquet, who was in practical matters Madame Guyon's closest friend, began to show signs of physical weakness, and grew steadily worse, until a few months later he died.

Meanwhile, the case against the Quietist movement, of

which Madame Guyon was erroneously supposed to be the representative, was continuing. There were plenty of people who were eager enough to prove her teaching to be wrong. Purity of life springing from the inner control of a holy God had no appeal to the sensual, pleasure-loving courtiers and ladies of Versailles. Their activities had already been greatly curtailed by the changed life of the King, who no longer indulged in illicit love affairs, but confined his attentions to Madame de Maintenon, now his secret though lawful wife. As he went tap-tap-tapping in his high-heeled shoes along the sumptuous, frescoed corridors of the palace to attend Mass, the members of his court followed him dutifully, but their carefully assumed expression of piety covered considerable irritation at his altered views on outward morality. If he got caught up in this new craze for spirituality as well, with its emphasis on the crucifixion of SELF and the enthronement of the Holy Spirit, life in Versailles simply would not be worth living. They had attended the ceremony, some years previously, when one of the King's mistresses, Louise de la Vallière, had taken the veil and disappeared for good into a convent, and the affair had provided an unusual and therefore welcome occasion for a court outing. It would be an entirely different matter if they were all expected to strive after a similar level of piety and self-control, even though not to the extent of entering monasteries and convents. They rebelled at the thought of having to exchange the gaiety of balls and theatres for religious meetings and prayer, flirtations and the festive cup for quiet studies of the Bible and the writings of the mystics, the thrill of the hunt for visits to the poor to improve their lot. In short, there was no lack of advocates at court for the suppression of 'Guyon-ism'. The ecclesiastics who were also against it had plenty of support from the high-born penitents who visited them for confession periodically, and duly obtained absolution. If between them it could be proved that Madame Guyon's teaching was false, it would be to their mutual satisfaction, though for different reasons.

Things came to such a pass that the Dukes of Beauvilliers and Chevreuse and the Abbé Fenelon again decided some action must be taken to clear her and vindicate her teaching. Their loyal plan to present her case to the King having been rejected, they came up with a different suggestion. Since it was her teaching that was being condemned, let her apply to the man whose opinion in these matters would be most highly respected, and ask him to examine her writings.

To this she agreed. It seemed to be a good idea. If anything she had written was contrary to the accepted doctrines of the Church, she would willingly alter it, although she had gone through it all before, with other theologians.

And so the day came when a new figure entered the scene, one who was to play a decisive role in the drama of her life. The Duke of Chevreuse brought to meet her Bossuet, the Bishop of Meaux.

A Little Bird I Am

A little bird I am,
　　Shut from the fields of air:
And in my cage I sit and sing
　　To Him who placed me there;
Well-pleased a prisoner to be,
Because, my God, it pleases Thee.

Nought have I else to do;
　　I sing the whole day long;
And He, whom most I love to please,
　　Doth listen to my song.
He caught and bound my wandering wing,
But still He bends to hear me sing.

Thou hast an ear to hear,
　　A heart to love and bless;
And though my notes were e'er so rude,
　　Thou shouldst not hear the less;
Because Thou knowest, as they fall,
That Love, sweet Love, inspires them all.

My cage confines me round,
　　Abroad I cannot fly;
But though my wing is closely bound,
　　My heart's at liberty.
My prison walls cannot control
The flight, the freedom of the soul.

O! It is good to soar
　　These bolts and bars above,
To Him whose purpose I adore,
　　Whose providence I love;
And in Thy mighty will to find
The joy, the freedom of the mind.

Jeanne de la Mothe Guyon,
written in the Prison of Vincennes.

11

To the Bastille

If Madame Guyon had any natural apprehensions about an interview with the most prominent churchman of the day, the preacher who could hold his listeners spellbound, the controversialist who could prove his point in the fiercest theological debates, those apprehensions were speedily dispelled. The Bishop was genial and reassuring. Some years ago he had read her little book on prayer and also her commentary on the Song of Solomon, he told her, and thought them very good. He was not at all opposed to inward religion – quite the reverse.

'This prelate said to us such strong things on the interior way and the authority of God over the soul, that I was surprised. He gave us even examples of persons he had known, whom he deemed saints, that had killed themselves. I confess I was startled by all this talk of the Bishop of Meaux. I knew that in the primitive Church some virgins had caused their own deaths in order to keep themselves pure; but I did not believe, in this age, where there is neither violence nor tyrants, a man could be approved for such an action.' She knew, at any rate, that nothing she had written contained such strange sentiments, and had no hesitation in letting him see all the books she had written, whether printed or still in manuscript form. She wanted to conceal nothing. She wanted him to know the reasons for her faith and convictions, and in order that he might the better understand her and the experience through which she had passed, she went further, giving him something she had never intended for publication.

She gave him her autobiography. All she asked was that it should be treated with the secrecy of the confessional.

It is difficult to understand what prompted her to give

such an intimate and uninhibited revelation of her experiences, practical and mystical, into the hands of a man she had never before met. The trustfulness of the action is evidence of her naiveté, and of her complete confidence in Bossuet himself. Her best friends had introduced him as being the one most likely to give her a fair hearing, and his kindly attitude towards her was disarming. Humanly speaking, she saw no reason for withholding it.

'At that time I flattered myself (though I accused myself of my faithlessness) that he would support me against those who were attacking me. But how far was I from knowing him! And how subject to error is that which one does not see in God's light, and which He does not Himself disclose!'

Bossuet took the enormous bundle of writings off with him, and some days later intimated to the Duke of Chevreuse that he had found in what he read 'an unction he had found nowhere else'. It was all very encouraging. They were not to know that he declared elsewhere that his stomach was turned again and again as he read her books. The intuitions, the visions and the interpretations put on them in her younger days which he now read were too much for him. To a literal-minded man with no bent for mysticism, they made no appeal.

Several months passed before he did anything more about them, but early in 1690 he made an arrangement to meet her and discuss what she had written.

The interview was a disaster from her point of view. Bossuet arrived at it with twenty carefully planned objections, and brought them out so vehemently that she was taken aback. She managed to answer some of his criticisms correctly. 'God assisted me, so that I satisfied him on everything that had relation to the dogma of the Church and the purity of doctrine,' she recorded, but continued, 'But there were some passages on which I could not satisfy him. As he spoke with extreme vigour, and hardly gave me time to explain my thoughts, it was not possible for me to make him change upon some of those articles, as I had done on others. We separated very late, and I left that conference with a head so exhausted, and in such a state of prostration, I was ill from it for several days.'

Some of the passages that the Bishop of Meaux objected to were not in her published writings, but in the autobiography she had so trustingly handed to him. According to him, she saw herself as the Woman in the Apocalypse, and made all sorts of claims beyond what the greatest saints would claim, regarding her relationship to God.

'The Bishop of Meaux raised great objections to what I said in my *Life*, of the Apostolic state. What I have meant to say is that persons who, by their state and condition (as, for instance, laymen and women) are not called upon to aid souls, ought not to intrude into it of themselves; but when God wished to make use of them by His authority, it was necessary they should be put into the state of which I have spoken. . . That this state is possible we have only to open the histories of all times to show that God has made use of laymen and women to instruct, edify, conduct and bring souls to a very high perfection. . . . "He has chosen weak things to confound the strong." '

There can be little doubt that those few hours of mental battering had a profound effect on Madame Guyon – perhaps rather a salutary one. Until that time it had seemed to her unnecessary to define the meaning of what she had written on the spur of the moment. Now that she had to explain what she meant, she was hard put to it to do so.

'I have a defect, which is that I say things as they occur to me, without knowing whether I speak well or ill; while I am saying or writing them they appear to me clear as day; after that I see them as things I have not known, far from having written them. Nothing remains in my mind but a void. . .'

If the Bishop of Meaux had been prepared to discuss things quietly, and had given her time to explain herself, the interview would have been much more to her satisfaction. As it was, all she could do was to pursue him with letters, endeavouring to clarify the points he had raised, which she had been too bewildered to answer at the time. Although he eventually responded kindly enough, assuring her that he found nothing in her that was not Catholic, he also intimated that there were certain views she held with which he could not agree.

'I am ready to believe that my imaginations are mixed up as shadows with the divine truth, which may indeed conceal it, but cannot injure it. I pray God with all my heart to crush me by the most terrible means, rather than I should rob Him of the least of His glory,' she wrote.

This whole episode shook her badly. It raised questions in her own mind as to whether she had inadvertently misled others. She could not guarantee that she had never been deceived, she wrote to the Duke of Beauvilliers, but she called him to witness that she had never done so intentionally. As for being proud, as the Bishop had implied – well, maybe she was, since she knew she was capable of anything bad! 'But the fire will purify all. I can very well believe I may have been mistaken, but I cannot complain nor be afflicted at all.' She took comfort, she said, in the fact that God was not less great, less perfect, or less happy for all her errors. As for herself, 'It appears to me I am below all creatures, a veritable nothing.'

During this period she lived a very secluded life in a small house in Paris, knowing little of what was going on outside except what Monsieur Fouquet told her. It was through him that she learned of the fantastic stories being circulated about her by Sister Rose and others. Her first reaction seems to have been to creep away altogether. She was obviously feeling very depressed when she wrote to the Duke of Chevreuse that she must 'once more become a wanderer, without hearth or home, ill and abandoned by all the world', but that since God evidently intended it, she consented to it with all her heart. She would disappear into a village where no one knew her, and live like a peasant!

Her little group of influential friends evidently protested against this idea, and, in fact, she gave it up herself. To run away now would be tantamount to admitting that the rumours had some truth in them, and she realised that if her morals were brought into question, it would reflect on her teaching. Instead of following her natural inclination to be done with it all, therefore, she did exactly the opposite. She wrote to Madame de Maintenon, explaining that as long as she was only accused of praying and teaching others to do so, she had remained in obscurity. 'But learning I am accused of things which touch honour, and that they speak of crimes, I thought it due to the Church, to my family, and to myself, that the truth should be known.' Then she went on to ask to have her case investigated by men of recognised integrity, half of them to be ecclesiastics, half laymen, in order that her morals as well as her theology should be brought to the light of day. This, she felt, was a justice refused to no one, and she added that while her case was under review she would go with the maid who had served her for fourteen years to any prison the King should indicate.

The reply she received from Madame de Maintenon really upset her, although on the face of it it appeared reasonable enough. It was given through the Duke de Beauvilliers, who had acted as go-between.

'Madame de Maintenon answered him that she had never believed any of the rumours that were circulated as to my morals; that she believed them very good. But it was my doctrine that was bad – that in justifying my morals, it was to be feared currency might be given to my sentiments, that it might be in some way to authorise them. And it was better, once and for all, to search out what related to doctrine, after which the rest would of itself drop.'

So once again there was to be an examination of her writings and teaching, but this time in the full glare of publicity, and with the scurrilous rumours about her allowed to persist unchallenged!

'They tried to tarnish my morals to tarnish my faith. I wished to justify the morals to justify the faith. They will not have it. What more can I do?' she wrote rather desperately. 'If they condemn me they cannot for that remove me from the bosom of the Church, my mother, since I condemn all she could condemn in my writings. I cannot admit having had thoughts I never had, nor having committed crimes I have not even known, far from committing them; because this would be to lie to the Holy Ghost. And like as I am ready to die for the faith and the decisions of the Church, I am ready to die to maintain that I have not thought what they insist I thought when writing, and that I have not committed the crimes they impute to me.' She was prepared to submit to the authority of the Church if she was ordered to refrain from teaching and writing. This prohibition she accepted, but beyond that she could not go.

It was at this time that she made a serious mistake, which was to cost her very dear. The Archbishop of Paris himself sent her a message that he had received a number of false memoirs about her, and asked her to come and see him. He would extricate her from her troubles, he said.

'He would have fully justified me, according to what I have since learned on good authority,' she wrote. 'I owe this justice to the fidelity of my God, that He did not fail me on this occasion, and that He put it into my heart to go to him. I even believed myself obliged to obey the voice of my Shepherd; but my friends . . . did not allow me to go, nor follow the inclination I had.'

Now her friends had their reasons. The Archbishop's offer of help was prompted by no concern for Madame Guyon, nor any particular approval of her teaching, but mainly because he cordially disliked the Bishop of Meaux, that upstart who was gaining altogether too much influence at Court and in ecclesiastical matters! If he, as Archbishop, intervened in this affair, he would be proving his superior ecclesiastical authority.

But behind the Bishop of Meaux, in the shadows, was the powerful figure of Madame de Maintenon, who had secretly authorised the commission. Political as well as ecclesiastical forces were at work, and Madame Guyon's friends, with the best intentions, persuaded her not to accept the Archbishop's invitation. Not surprisingly he was extremely annoyed, and forthwith banned her writings.

So the investigation went ahead in what came to be known as the Issy Conferences. For months Bossuet, Bishop of

Meaux, took time off from his full and busy life to meet de Noailles, Bishop of Chalons, and the highly respected old Monsieur Tronson, and for hours at a time the three of them discussed what Madame Guyon meant by what she said. This led them on to examine such obscure theological subjects as whether or not it was possible for a devout soul to love God so selflessly as to be prepared to spend eternity in the torments of hell, if He so willed it. A hypothetical question based on an impossibility, some might have called it, but at any rate it revealed the diligence with which they applied themselves to the task in hand. Pure love had to be accurately defined, and since Madame Guyon had raised the matter by something she had ecstatically written, it should be gone into.

If the Bishop of Meaux had had his way, she would have been condemned outright as a heretic and a dangerous woman, but she had an unexpected advocate in the aged Monsieur Tronson, who had taken the trouble to make enquiries on his own account about her conduct and character. From the Bishops of Geneva, Grenoble and Turin came the same report in varying degrees of enthusiasm. Her moral character was beyond reproach, her generosity to the poor was outstanding, and the influence she had had on a large number of people had been for good, and drawn them nearer to God. In the face of such testimonies it was difficult to designate her as a dangerous woman, and since she had made it quite clear she renounced anything that was contrary to the doctrines of the Church, she could scarcely be branded as a heretic. When it came to the crunch, they could find nothing in her doctrine that was contrary to what was already accepted in the Church. So the Issy Conferences eventually came to a conclusion with the production of some thirty articles of elementary faith, all of which she believed and subscribed to without difficulty. What disturbed her was that their production had ever seemed necessary, implying, as she thought, that 'those given to prayer believed neither in God nor in Jesus Christ'. She saw them as an indirect indictment of her teaching. However, they were seen in a different light by one who might have been as hurt as she by their publication. Somehow Father La Combe, in his imprisonment in Lourdes, got wind of the affair, and managed to send a reassuring letter to her in which he emphasised the importance of such orthodox truths as the articles contained being absolutely safeguarded. There was nothing for her to be worried about. She had done quite right to sign them. As a woman she was not expected to solve theological debates. Whatever may have happened to Father La Combe a few years later, he was evidently in his right mind when he wrote that letter.

By this time Madame Guyon was no longer living in Paris, but in a convent in the diocese of the Bishop of Meaux. The censure of her books by the Archbishop of Paris after her refusal to see him had made the place too hot for her, and trustingly she had agreed to Bossuet's suggestion that she should make her temporary home with the nuns of St. Mary.

In all but one way it proved a good move for her, and not so good for him. The nuns may have been prejudiced against her before they met her, but she won them over completely. Her arrival one night in mid-winter, having spent some hours in a snow drift, alone with her maid in a carriage abandoned by the driver, was dramatic, but half-frozen as they were the two women made no complaint. During the six months she remained with them there was perfect harmony between the devout, orthodox nuns of St. Mary and their visitor who was suspected of heresy.

The nuns saw another side of their usually benign and urbane Bishop, too, for he came one day when Madame Guyon was recovering from an illness, and really bullied her. He wanted her to sign a document in which it was implied she had fallen into some of the religious errors that the Church condemned. He was quite genial about it at first, but when she explained mildly that she could not do that, he spoke more vehemently, but to no effect. The quieter her voice as she answered him, the louder his voice became, and the Prioress, standing by, was dismayed to observe that the Bishop was in danger of losing his temper.

It was a disturbing scene, one that was enacted several times during Madame Guyon's stay in the convent, and one day, the Bishop having gone again without getting his way, the Prioress said to Madame Guyon, 'You ought not to have answered him so gently. If people stand up to him he calms down, but if they don't he raves on. It's his nature.' But it was not Madame Guyon's nature to be otherwise than gentle, whether verbally attacked by a bad-tempered mother-in-law or an angry Bishop. The Prioress was cast in a different mould, and on at least one occasion protested strongly to the Bishop at the way he was treating this resident in her convent. He admitted then that, having thoroughly examined the writings of Madame Guyon, he had found nothing wrong except some terminology not completely orthodox, 'but a woman is not expected to be a theologian.' With which sentiment, of course, everyone agreed. He further intimated that he was being egged on to extract a confession of heresy from her by people in a very powerful position.

No names were mentioned, but when Madame Guyon heard of it she had little difficulty in identifying one of them. It was Madame de Maintenon. Bossuet was making no empty boast when, discussing the affair with the Prioress, he said, in an unguarded moment, 'This business will gain for me the Archbishopric of Paris or a Cardinal's hat!' He was working for promotion, and aiming high. 'But God won't allow him to have the one or the other,' said Madame Guyon confidently, when the Prioress told her what he had said. And in that prophecy she proved to be right.

Interestingly enough, it was the man who was unobtrusively supporting her, Fenelon himself, who obtained an archbishopric. The See of Cambrai, on France's northeastern border, fell vacant about this time, and Fenelon was nominated as successor to the Spanish archbishop who had just died. This did not mean he would spend much time there. The appointment was not to be allowed to interfere with his duties as tutor to the young Duc de Bourgogne. He would remain at court for part of the year, only visiting

Cambrai when convenient. Viewed from a worldly and financial point of view, this was definitely preferment. Fenelon, though an aristocrat, was a poor man, with only one small benefice, but he immediately surrendered that on his appointment – to the surprise of some of his fellow-clerics who saw no harm in the quiet retention of such wealth as came their way. One archbishop, on hearing of it, remarked drily that Fenelon, thinking as he did, had acted well in surrendering his benefice, and that he himself, thinking as he did, had also acted well in keeping all of his. Let each man act according to his convictions!

This appointment, which put Fenelon on an equal footing with Bossuet, did nothing to improve relations between the two men. All the same, it may have influenced Bossuet to modify his attitude towards Madame Guyon, since Fenelon was known to approve of her teaching. Whatever may have been the reason, having failed to extract from her a confession that she did not believe in the virgin birth, and that she and Father La Combe had both taught heresy, he eventually gave up trying to force it from her. (The Madame Guyon who confronted him with such firmness was a very different Madame Guyon from the browbeaten young bride who had tried to win over an insolent servant with meekly-proffered presents.) Instead, after she had been in the convent about six months, he presented her with a testimonial which was of such importance that she sent it to her family for safe keeping. It read as follows:

'We, Bishop of Meaux, certify to all whom it may concern that, by means of the declarations and submission of Madame Guyon which we have before us subscribed with her hand, and the prohibitions accepted by her with submission, of writing, teaching, dogmatising in the Church, or of spreading her books printed or manuscript, or of conducting souls in the ways of prayer, or otherwise: together with the good testimony that has been furnished us during six months that she is in our diocese and in the convent of St. Mary, we are satisfied with her conduct, and have continued to her the participation of the Holy Sacraments in which we have found her; we declare, besides, we have not found her implicated in any way in the abominations of Molinos or others elsewhere condemned, and we have not intended to comprehend her in the mention which has been made by us of them in our Ordinance of April 6th, 1695: given at Meaux, July 1st, 1695.'

A few days later she was given another testimonial, hand-written, a copy of which had been given to Bossuet. It must have touched her as it must touch the thoughtful reader in the twentieth century, coming down the corridors of time as a sort of memorial to three unknown but courageous and loyal women who did what they could to stand for the truth. This is what she read:

'We, the undersigned, Superior and nuns of the Visitation of St. Mary of Meaux, certify that Madame Guyon, having lived in our House by the order and permission of the Bishop of Meaux, our illustrious Prelate and Superior, for the space of six months, she has not given us any cause for trouble or annoyance, but much of edification; having never spoken to a person within or without except with special permission; having, besides, neither received nor written anything except as the Bishop has permitted her; having observed in all her conduct and all her words a great regularity, simplicity, sincerity, humility, mortification, sweetness, and Christian patience, and a true devotion and esteem of all that is of the faith, especially in the mystery of the Incarnation and Holy Childhood of our Lord Jesus Christ. That if the said lady wished to choose our House to live there the rest of her days in retirement, our Community would deem it a favour and gratification. This protest is simple and sincere, without other view or thought than to bear witness to the truth. Signed. Sister Françoise Elizabeth le Picard, Superior, Sister Magdalen Amy Gueton, Sister Claude Marie Amouri, July 7th, 1695.'

There were times when, in her distress, Madame Guyon wrote of being 'abandoned by all the world', when, like Elijah, she saw herself as the only one left who was faithful to the revelation of the God whose Kingdom is in the human heart. And, like Elijah, she was wrong. In the France of the seventeenth century, as in Israel hundreds of years before Christ, God had His hidden ones who would not bow the knee to any Baal.

As there was now no reason for Madame Guyon to remain in the convent, she asked and obtained permission from the Bishop to leave, and departed with two friends who came to escort her to their home. The testimonial he had given her would answer any further accusations about her doctrine, it seemed, though the rumours about her moral character continued to circulate. She had in her possession letters from Cardinal Camus and a Benedictine Prior, both of Grenoble, both testifying to her purity of conduct, but there was no way in which she could use them to vindicate herself. She read them over sometimes, those reassuring words, written by the indignant Prior denying that he had ever supported foul accusations against her.

'. . . fabricate a calumny against you! and they made me the instrument of it! I never thought what they put in my mouth, nor of making the complaints of which they pretend I am the author. I declare, on the contrary, and I have already many times declared, that I have never heard of you anything but what is very Christian and very honourable. I should have taken good care not to see you, Madame, if I had believed you capable of saying what I would not dare to write, and what the Apostle forbids us to name. If it is, however, necessary to your justification I should name it, I will do it on the first notion, and I will distinctly say there is nothing of the kind, that I have never heard you say anything similar, nor anything which has the least resemblance to it . . . They have already written to me on the subject, and I have already given the same answer. I would do it a thousand times more if I were asked a thousand times.' Let her apply to him again, if necessary, and he would bear testimony to the truth. He would not wound his conscience by a cowardly silence!

If she had been allowed to defend herself in a court of law, she knew she had sufficient evidence and convincing witnesses to prove her innocence. As it was, she was denied that privilege. Hers was deemed a case for the ecclesiastical authorities only. The testimonials she had received, which in a free country in the twentieth century would have made headline news in the media, could not be made public, and in a matter of days the most important one, that given her by Bossuet, had to be secreted to preserve it, for he sent to demand its return. And through the Prioress he ordered, not only the return of the testimonial, but the return of Madame Guyon to the convent.

With that demand, sent on by the Prioress, came a private letter from the courageous woman herself. 'Don't obey the command,' was the gist of what she said in it. 'Things will be even worse for you if you fall into the Bishop's hands again. Much as we want to have you with us here, we'd rather you stayed away for your own sake.' Madame Guyon understood. The Bishop had offended Madame de Maintenon, in whose eyes he had slipped up badly in giving her that testimonial, and agreeing to her leaving the convent. Now he was trying to retrieve the mistake. The one way in which her move to the convent did not prove good for her was that by doing so she had placed herself under his jurisdiction. When she did not obey the order to return, he gave out that she had left without his permission, by escaping over the convent wall.

Madame Guyon had escaped from the convent of St. Mary in Meaux over the garden wall! So the rumour got around, and she knew the net was closing about her. Unwilling to involve her family and friends in her disgrace, she declined invitations from two or three of them to retreat quietly into their homes in the country, and set off secretly with her maid for Paris. Once there, she went into hiding.

'As I was informed my enemies were about to push things with the utmost violence, I believed I should leave to God all that should happen, and yet take all prudent steps to avoid the effect of the menaces that reached me from all sides.' She rented a cheap apartment in a secluded tenement, staying indoors the whole time while her maid went quietly out of a side door for the necessary shopping, and to bring back what news she could.

Rumours abounded about the notorious Madame Guyon who had so mysteriously disappeared.

Lieutenant le Gres had orders to find her.

The police were searching for her everywhere!

She was to be arrested and tried – then she would have her head chopped off!

No – she was to be burned at the stake, and her ashes scattered to the four winds!

She managed to get letters out to her friends occasionally, and in one to the Duke of Beauvilliers she referred quite humorously to the threats of execution, asserting that they had delighted her for a whole day, and that she couldn't wait for her ashes to be flying. The very thought of it just suited her, she said. It is probable that her friends were having a worse time of it in some ways than she herself, for they knew what was going on.

Worst of all, they knew what was being said, and the way in which Madame Guyon was being ridiculed. Bossuet, unable to find ways of convicting her of heresy, had made her the butt for vulgar jokes instead, and he had used her own autobiography to do it.

That autobiography, written when she was younger, and with the extravagance of thought and expression which came naturally to her, had been given to him on the one condition that he treated it with the secrecy of the confessional. She had been assailed by doubts as to the wisdom of letting him see it after she had done so, and sent a message asking for its return, but he retained it for months before letting her have it back, and by that time he had assimilated its contents. Some of the things she had written were quite intimate, for she had never intended it for publication, but had obeyed the instructions of Father La Combe, her spiritual director, to write exactly what she had experienced. One little incident in particular the Bishop of Meaux remembered, and now made full use of. She had been present on an occasion when a group of people were discussing some passage in the Bible, and she realised they were putting the wrong interpretation on its meaning. This distressed her. Too reticent to dispute the point, she kept quiet, but was so overcome with suppressed emotion that she started panting and it seemed she was likely to faint. Then it was, as she wrote quite frankly in her autobiography, her tight-fitting bodice and stays had to be loosened, and on this trivial intimate detail the Bishop of Meaux fastened. 'She was so overcome she had to loosen her stays . . .' One can imagine how the corridors of Versailles would ring with laughter as the phrase was taken up in suggestive conversation, and in whatever context it was used, Madame Guyon was the name attached to it. The Bishop of Meaux may have failed to produce evidence to prove her a heretic, but he succeeded in making her an object of ribaldry. The little group of those at court who were known to be loyal to her had to endure that shame. It is sometimes harder to stand by someone who is being laughed at than someone who is being opposed.

If Madame Guyon was conscious that the net was being drawn around her, the Duke of Beauvilliers, in charge of the household of the Dauphin's children, and Fenelon as their tutor, had good cause to suspect that it was also being spread for them. Their names were so closely associated with hers that any action taken against her would inevitably affect them.

There was a sort of lull during the months in which she was successfully evading the unjust arrest awaiting her. No less an impartial witness to the whole affair than the aged Monsieur Tronson got a message to her confirming her in remaining out of sight, assuring her that she had good reason for doing so. But the period of quietness and comparative comfort in her own little home came to an end when her place of hiding was discovered. This happened two days after Christmas, 1695. Her maid, out on an errand, was recognised and followed home. The police entered the house, arrested Madame Guyon, and with her maid she was taken to the castle in the forest of Vincennes, near Paris, and there imprisoned.

Simple Trust

Still, still, without ceasing,
  I feel it increasing,
This fervour of holy desire;
  And often exclaim,
  Let me die in the flame
Of a love that can never expire!

  Had I words to explain
  What she must sustain
Who dies to the world and its ways;
  How joy and affright,
  Distress and delight,
Alternately chequer her days.

  Thou, sweetly severe;
  I would make Thee appear
In all Thou art pleased to award,
  Not more in the sweet,
  Than the bitter I meet,
My tender and merciful Lord.

  Thus Faith, in the dark
  Pursuing its mark
Through many sharp trials of Love;
  Is the sorrowful waste
  That is to be passed
In the way to the Canaan above.

Jeanne de la Mothe Guyon

12

It does not end here

Fenelon, Archbishop of Cambrai, was in a predicament, and Bossuet, Bishop of Meaux, intended to keep him in it. It had been at the instigation of the Bishop that Madame Guyon was incarcerated in Vincennes, and he was determined that the Archbishop should agree that he had done right. The woman must be branded as a heretic, thus vindicating him in the eyes of all for the action he had taken against her, and, incidentally satisfying Madame de Maintenon on whose approval so much depended. The difficulty was that the Archbishop did not see eye to eye with him, and the Archbishop was very highly esteemed in some influential quarters. It was a complicated situation, needing tactful handling, but it had to be done, so the Bishop set about it in an oblique manner.

He did not demand of the Archbishop public support of his action, open agreement that Madame Guyon's teaching was contrary to that of the Church. Instead, he wrote a book.

His ostensible purpose in writing the book was an admirable one, and the subject he chose was thoroughly relevant to the current ecclesiastical preoccupation. In other words, it was topical. It dealt with the whole matter of mystical prayer and the inner life as practised and recommended by such recently canonised saints as St. Francis de Sales, Saint Teresa, and St. John of the Cross, not to mention those of earlier vintage. And Bossuet, Bishop of Meaux, wrote as an ardent advocate of the subject. If it had not been a topic of major concern to him before, it evidently was now. He wrote of it in all its varied stages and aspects. Certainly he was in favour of prayer, and an inner life in union with God! What he feared, what he deplored, what he was opposed to, was the introduction of dangerous errors and heresies like those of Molinos and the Quietists. These were what should be guarded against. Having written the book he sent it to Fenelon, his old pupil and erstwhile friend, for his approval. If that could be obtained the breach between them would be seen to be healed and he, the Bishop, would be seen to have been in the right.

But Fenelon, after glancing at the manuscript, politely refused to read it. His reason? He had detected in the margins quotations from Madame Guyon's writings which were produced as examples of the Quietist heresies. As he explained to the Duke of Chevreuse, his friend, he saw immediately that the book was a covert attack on her own little publication *A Short Method of Prayer*, and he was quite unwilling to add his name to what amounted to a condemnation of her. The least he could do for one of his friends in adversity, in whose integrity he had complete confidence, was to keep silent while others condemned, he said. It would be simpler to return the book unread than to read it and refuse to approve it, so would the Duke kindly act on his behalf by returning the manuscript promptly to the Bishop, and explaining his reason for doing so?

The Duke, who understood the situation completely, accepted the charge, and no doubt came in for a display of the Bishop's displeasure as he expressed himself amazed, shocked, indeed scandalised at the Archbishop's attitude, creating as it did an open breach between them. The leading ecclesiastics in France seen to be at variance! What damage it would do to the Church! And all over a pockmarked widow who fancied herself as a prophetess! If the Bishop did not put it in exactly those words, that is no doubt what he meant.

But the Archbishop was adamant. He did not deny that Madame Guyon was given to exaggeration, and that she expressed herself imperfectly, but he knew her personally, and her basic faith as well as her practice was entirely conformable to Catholic doctrine. In any case, her writings had already been passed by one lot of theologians and then by another, she had accepted with the utmost docility all the corrections they had suggested, so what was there to complain about?

That is as far as he went in open defence of her, but like the Benedictine Prior of Grenoble, he refused to wound his own conscience by a cowardly silence. He used the same method as the Bishop.

He, too, wrote a book.

He called it *The Maxims of the Saints*, and although he did not mention her name, it included and expressed more clearly than Madame Guyon herself had done her teaching on the inner life. And as he was a rapid writer, and his book was shorter, the Duke of Chevreuse rushed it through the press and got it into the hands of readers six weeks ahead of the publication of the Bishop's more ponderous work.

It all caused as great a flare-up as the proverbial fat when it gets into the fire. Those who were not intimately involved were outwardly appalled and inwardly delighted at the prospect of a row between leading prelates in the Church. Those who knew what lay behind it were alarmed, and as for the Bishop himself, he was furious. Madame de Maintenon, knowing he had the sympathetic ear of King Louis himself, made one or two ineffectual attempts to calm the situation that she herself had been largely responsible for bringing about, for she still had a deep respect and affection for Fenelon, but her efforts were in vain. The King had his own reason for disliking Fenelon (Fenelon had rebuked him strongly on one occasion for his indifference to the sufferings of his own people brought on by his ambitious wars) and was willing enough to listen to Bossuet's accusation against him.

The Bishop, of course, went about it in the correct manner. He approached His Most Christian Majesty in a penitent attitude, asking for his forgiveness, and then explained that there was something he ought to have revealed before. It was about the Archbishop of Cambrai. The Bishop feared that his fellow-prelate was becoming very fanatical. The fact was, he had serious leanings towards the heresies of the Quietists, having come under the influence of Madame Guyon. He was thus a danger to the Church and also to the Crown, for was he not the tutor to His Majesty's grandson, the Duc de Bourgogne, second heir to the throne? What insidious heresies might not be spread throughout the court and then the realm through the influence of the Archbishop of Cambrai! Could His Majesty forgive him, the Bishop, for not having revealed this earlier?

His Most Christian Majesty expressed himself horrified at what he heard, and was thoroughly worked up about it. He graciously forgave the Bishop, as Bossuet of course knew he would, but made it plain that something must be done about Fenelon, as Bossuet, of course, intended that it should.

And so the gathering storm broke. Fenelon appealed to Rome, requesting that his book should be scrutinised there, to receive from the Pope's ultimate authority either the Papal approval or condemnation. He wanted to go to Rome in person, to present his case himself, but for that he needed the King's permission to leave France, and this was summarily refused. He must not cross the French border. The seventeenth-century equivalent of the twentieth-century exit visa was as difficult to obtain, in certain cases, as it often is now. On the contrary, he was ordered to leave the capital and return to his remote diocese of Cambrai *and remain there.* This was tantamount to telling him he could no longer hold the position of tutor to the second heir to the throne. He was virtually dismissed. Not even the heartfelt plea of the King's own grandson, the young Duc de Bourgogne, on behalf of his beloved teacher, could move the King to alter his decision. The purity of the Catholic Faith was at stake, he told the boy piously, and therefore he could not grant personal favours. He must defend the Faith at all costs.

Bent on rooting out 'Guyonism' as he called it, he turned his attention to St. Cyr, where it had flourished for a time. He went personally to the place, got the local Bishop to condemn all Madame Guyon's writings found there, and had three of the staff members known to be loyal to Madame Guyon turned out. At the same time her younger son was stripped of his commission in the army.

The King did not stop there, either. Bossuet saw to that. His activity was now directed towards Rome. The Pope must be persuaded to condemn in the strongest measure *The Maxims of the Saints*, and thereby finally crush the Archbishop of Cambrai. So started the series of intrigues and consultations, the urgent messages and the covert threats, the flood of literature that made headline news in court and Church circles in France and Italy, which threatened to bring the King of France and the Pope into open conflict.

Meanwhile, the innocent cause of all the trouble was locked up in prison, writing poetry.

*   *   *

What would have been a shattering experience for most women of her upbringing had no apparent adverse effect on the spirits of Madame Guyon. She had long ago learned to endure physical hardship and natural privations, had a mind armed with a willingness to suffer, and entered prison with all the poise of the martyr prepared to die for her cause. So far from being appalled by the conditions into which she entered, she appeared thoroughly to enjoy the first few months in Vincennes. She had longed for isolation from the world, and the freedom to devote herself to quiet meditation, prayer, adoration and worship – now she had got it. If the room in which she was incarcerated was cold and damp, it was rendered as comfortable as her devoted maid-servant, who shared it with her, could make it. Her rank was respected to the extent of being allowed to have a few pieces of her own furniture in it, and she was not deprived of pen and paper. She wrote of her time in Vincennes quite glowingly:

'During the time I was at Vincennes and Monsieur de la Reinie interrogated me, I continued in great peace, very content to pass my life there, if such was the will of God. I used to compose hymns, which the maid who served me learned by heart as fast as I composed them; and we used to sing Your praise, O my God! I regarded myself as a little bird You were keeping in a cage for Your pleasure, and who ought to sing to fulfil her condition of life. The stones of my tower seemed to me rubies; that is to say, I esteemed them more than all worldly magnificence. My joy was based on Your Love, O my God, and on the pleasure of being Your captive; although I made these reflections only when composing hymns. The depth of my heart was full of that joy which You give to those who love You, in the midst of the greatest crosses.'

There was one occasion, however, when that peace was spoiled, and she blamed her own faithlessness for it.

'I was considering beforehand one day, the answers that I should make to an interrogation that I was to be subjected to the next day. I answered it all astray. And God, so faithful, who had made me answer difficult and perplexed matters with much facility and presence of mind . . . permitted that on this occasion I could with difficulty answer the most simple things, and that I remained almost without knowing what to say. This infidelity of mine spoiled my peace for some days; but it soon returned, and I believe, my Lord, that You permitted this fault only to make me see the uselessness of our arrangements on such occasions, and the security of trusting ourselves to You. Those who still depend upon human reasoning will say, we must look beforehand and arrange; and that it is to tempt God and to expect miracles, to act otherwise. I let others think what they please; for myself, I find security only in abandoning myself to the Lord. All Scripture is full of testimonies which demand this abandonment. "Make over your trouble to the hand of the Lord; He will act Himself. Abandon yourself to His conduct; and He will Himself conduct your steps." God has not meant to set snares for us in telling us this, and in teaching us not to premeditate our answers.'

However, after a few months she was removed from Vincennes to a convent in Vaugirard, a village near Paris, and here she was not so happy. She preferred the gaolers to the nuns, she told the Duke of Chevreuse in a letter. Her maid-servant was left behind in Vincennes, and the convent regime proved harsher than that of the prison. It was here, too, that the final attempt was made to discredit her in the eyes of the world.

Her relationship with Father La Combe, who had been a prisoner for ten years by this time, again came under review, and with 'fresh evidence' which she was called upon to answer. She had become accustomed to interrogations by this time, but the one she had to face in Vaugirard was the worst of them all. The local Curé, who had hitherto conducted them, was accompanied this time by an Archbishop Noailles, and confronted her with a letter purporting to have been written by Father La Combe from the prison in Vincennes, where he had now been taken. It was addressed to her – but it had first got into the hands of Bossuet, who had had copies made of it and circulated them. La Combe's letter called upon her to confess, as he was now doing, the misdemeanours and sins of their relationship, to repent of them, and henceforth to live a penitent and blameless life . . . The implication that they had indulged in immoral practices was unmistakable.

'Let me see the letter,' Madame Guyon said. 'It is probably a forgery.' She had had to defend herself against forgeries before. After scrutinising the letter she handed it back saying, 'If he wrote this it must have been under the torture.' Then she added slowly, 'Or else he has lost his reason.'

And that indeed was what had happened, though his insanity was not divulged at the time. He died some years later in a lunatic asylum. What had turned his brain, poisoned his sensitive imagination, must remain a secret until the Day when everything will be revealed.

It is doubtful whether even those most eager to do so really believed there was anything in Father La Combe's 'confessions'. Certainly Madame Guyon steadfastly refused to acknowledge there had ever been anything wrong in their relationship. She recollected that there had been one action which might have been misconstrued. She had once embraced him on his return from a long journey. There had never been anything beyond that. But it was her word against his – and against the array of powerful people, from the King down, who readily seized on the 'confessions' of a man who had been imprisoned for ten years before making them. They reflected on the morals of the friend whom Fenelon persisted in defending, the notable Madame Guyon, and therefore added further weight to the case being built up against him. Madame Guyon and what happened to her were now matters of secondary importance, although the scandal created through the 'confessions' was sufficient to land her eventually in the Bastille. But Fenelon was the central protagonist in the case now. Supported in the background by the Dukes of Beauvilliers and Chevreuse and their Duchesses, his most powerful antagonist was not now merely Bossuet, Bishop of Meaux, but the King himself, while the judge was the Pope. On his pronouncement Fenelon depended for the vindication of his teaching on what constituted pure love of God, and whether it is possible for man to attain it.

If the Pope, a man of over eighty, had been left to make the decision, the indications are that the final decision regarding *The Maxims of the Saints* would have been quite different from what it was. The political overtones of the situation, with the threat of a rupture between France and the Holy See if the King's demands were not met, evidently weighted the scales against Fenelon's book. In the event, the King's demands and Bossuet's deep desires were not met, for from their point of view the Brief of Condemnation that was eventually issued in March 1699, was not nearly strong enough. There was no mention in it of heresy, which was what they had hoped for – the book was merely condemned because it contained 'evil-sounding propositions' and the reading of it 'might lead the faithful insensibly into errors'. Privately the Pope served with a sigh that if Fenelon loved his God too much, Bossuet certainly loved his neighbour too little.

Nevertheless, the book was condemned, however mildly, and in the eyes of the world Fenelon had lost his battle.

It has well been said that crises do not make the man – they merely reveal him. The Papal verdict on his book, for which he had waited three years, reached Fenelon in his cathedral in Cambrai just as he was about to mount the pulpit and deliver a sermon. He stood still as he received the news, quietly absorbed it, then put aside the notes of the sermon he had prepared and quickly jotted down something else. Then he went up into the pulpit and preached, simply but eloquently, on the subject of submission. The text he chose was 'Thy will be done'. With complete self-possession and quiet dignity he made known the long-awaited result of the investigations into his book at Rome, accepted it meekly and with no evidence of bitterness, and went cheerfully about his business in the confines of his diocese for the rest of his life.

The curtain of history goes down at that point. The conflict was over. Bossuet was the victor, Fenelon, though still Archbishop of Cambrai, was 'disgraced', and as for Madame Guyon, she was reported to have died recently in the Bastille.

That finished it. Other matters occupied public attention, such as what would happen to the widespread empire of the weakly, childless Charles II of Spain when he died. And as he died the following year, and a few months later what went down in history as the war of the Spanish Succession broke out, the influence of the mysterious Madame Guyon was considered to be at an end.

But it was not.

In the first place, it was not she, but the maid-servant who had been imprisoned with her, who had died. In some ways this loyal woman had probably had a worse time of it than her mistress in prison, for not being of the same social rank she would have been treated with even less consideration. But she managed to get at least one letter smuggled out to her brother, which she wrote with a stick dipped in moist soot on paper that unexpectedly came her way, and it gave evidence that she had imbibed her mistress' spirit.

'Not a day passes that I do not thank God that He has imprisoned me here. I cannot forget the time when I laid myself upon His altar to be His in joy or in sorrow.' She regarded her imprisonment as the evidence that He had accepted her sacrifice. Then she went on to write of Madame Guyon:

'Having known her for twelve years, I think I know her thoroughly. It is an honour to share in her sufferings. It seems to me I have seen the divine nature manifested in her in a remarkable manner.

'We are now separated from each other. I am in this prison, she is in another, but we are still united in spirit. The walls of a prison may confine the body, but they cannot hinder the union of souls. It is the love of Christ that unites us . . .

'My dear brother, I do not go into details. I just say that she was an instrument in the hands of God to bring me to a knowledge of Himself – that God whom I now love and shall love for ever. She taught me the great lesson of self-denial, of dying to the life of nature, and of living only to the will of God. So do not wonder that I love her, because she and I love the same God.

'This love has the power of uniting our hearts in a way I cannot express; but it seems to me that it is the beginning of that union which we shall have in Heaven, where the love of God will unite us all in Him.'

She and Madame Guyon had lived and travelled together for so long that it is not surprising that a rumour of the death of one of them in prison should have led to the conclusion that it was the mistress, not the maid, who had gone. The fact that Madame Guyon was still alive became known when it was reported that she had again been interrogated by the Chief of Police, and that she had defended herself with great ability and firmness. Nothing could force from her a confession that she had done or deliberately taught anything contrary to the accepted doctrines of the Church of Rome. Eventually all efforts to do so were given up. Her health was failing, and it seemed likely that before long she would die in the Bastille, that notorious habitation of cruelty, to which she had been condemned. But in 1703 a strange turn of events took place. What induced His Most Christian Majesty to change his mind about the prisoner who had caused him so much disturbance in the court and the State is not quite clear, but the fact remains that he granted permission for her to be released from the Bastille and taken to Blois for a period of six months to recover her health – but only on the condition that she was kept under the strictest surveillance of her daughter and son-in-law who had an estate there, that she was to be allowed no communication with anyone else, and that if she was found doing so she would be returned to the Bastille immediately.

And so she emerged alive, one of the very few to do so, but silent as to what had happened to her within those thick, impregnable walls. Like everyone else who was taken there, she had had to promise on oath that she would never divulge what she saw or heard or endured there. All she ever revealed were a few sentences in her autobiography, written years later.

'When things were carried to the greatest extremity (I was then in the Bastille), and I learned of the defaming and horrible outcry against me, I said to You, O my God, "If You desire to make me a spectacle to men and angels, Your holy will be done. All that I ask of You is that You save those who are Yours, and do not permit them to separate themselves. Let not the powers, principalities, sword, etc., ever separate us from the love of God which is in Jesus Christ. For my own case, what matters it to me what men think of me? What matters it what they make me suffer, since they cannot separate me from Jesus Christ, who is implanted in the depth of my heart. If I displease Jesus Christ, though I should please all men, it would be less to me than the dirt." Let all men, therefore, despise me, hate me, provided I am agreeable to Him. Their blows will polish what is defective in me, in order that I may be presented to Him for whom I die every day until He comes to consume that death. And I prayed You, O my God, to make me an offering pure and clean in Your blood, soon to be offered to You.'

The worst times of all were when she felt that even God was against her. 'Sometimes it seemed God placed Himself on the side of men to make me suffer the more. I was then more exercised within than from outside. Everything was against me. I saw all men united to torment me and surprise me – every artifice and every subtlety of the intellect of men who have much of it, and who studied to that end; and I alone without help, feeling upon me the heavy hand of God, Who seemed to abandon me to myself and my own obscurity; and entire abandonment within, without being able to help myself with my natural intellect, whose entire vivacity was deadened this long time since I had ceased to make use of it, in order to allow myself to be led by a superior intellect; having laboured all my life to submit my mind to Jesus Christ and my reason to His guidance.'

Had that strong metaphysical tendency in her nature carried her away too far, depriving her of the ability to exercise the 'naked faith' of which she so often spoke when feelings were deadened? Or had she been brought to the last extremity, tasting the agony of Jesus Christ when he cried, 'My God, my God, why hast Thou forsaken me?' She did not analyse herself now, she merely recorded what she experienced in her soul during some of those dark, dark days in the Bastille.

'During this time I could not help myself, either with my reason or any interior support; for I was like those who have never experienced that admirable guidance from the goodness of God, and who have not natural intellect. When I prayed I had only answers of death. At this time that passage of David occurred to me; "When they persecuted me, I afflicted my soul by fasting".'

So she reverted to some of the old practices, fasting rigorously and inflicting penances, but all to no avail. 'All seemed to me like burned straw.' Then she added a simple, illuminating sentence, 'One moment of God's conducting is a thousand times more helpful.'

In one moment He could calm the agitated mind and revive drooping spirits, and He did not delay that liberating moment for any longer than was needful for the purifying fire of affliction to do its work. One afternoon in March 1703, she emerged from the Bastille to be taken to Blois, one hundred miles to the south-west of Paris, and there she remained for the rest of her life. The six month's leave was extended indefinitely, and although she suffered incessant physical infirmities and illnesses, she lived peacefully for another fourteen years without encountering any further opposition from the ecclesiastical authorities, though they evidently kept an eye on her.

'Take care what you say to so-and-so,' she was reminded from time to time, and when, after a friendly conversation, the visitor or visitors departed, she was told, 'You shouldn't have said that in front of those people! It could be misconstrued, and get you into trouble again. You really should be more careful! You are too naive.' She agreed she was too simple, but she could not help it, she replied. She couldn't be on her guard against anybody, and everything seemed to go off all right. 'O carnal prudence, how opposed I find you to the simplicity of Jesus Christ!' she wrote privately in her autobiography. 'I leave you to your partisans; as for me, my prudence, my wisdom, is Jesus, simple and little. Though I should be Queen by changing my conduct, I could not do it.' She was surprised to find that people liked to come and see her, and that whoever they were she seemed able to talk to them on their own level. 'God gives me a free air and makes me converse with people according to what they are, giving me even a natural cleverness with those who have it; and that, with an air so free, they go away pleased.' It must have been not unlike her early days in Grenoble, when people who had heard about her came to find out for themselves what was the secret of her piety and her prayerfulness and her quiet power.

They came from quite a distance, some of them – from England and Germany, the Protestant countries, as well as from her native France, and she received them all alike, speaking to them of Jesus Christ, the Divine Word. 'He alone is the truth. He said, "*Sanctify them in your truth. Your word is truth.*" He also said, "I sanctify Myself for them." Oh, how well these two things agree! To be sanctified in the truth is to have no other sanctity than that of Jesus Christ. May He alone be holy in us and for us. He will be holy in us when we shall be sanctified in His truth by that experimental knowledge that to Him alone belongs all sanctity, all justice, all strength, all greatness, all power, all glory; and to us, all poverty, weakness, etc. . . . .

'Jesus Christ will be holy for us, and will be to us everything. We shall find in Him all that is deficient in us. If we seek anything for ourselves out of Him, if we seek anything in us as *ours*, however holy it may appear to us, we are liars, and the truth is not in us. We seduce ourselves . . .'

It was the same message with which she herself had commenced her spiritual pilgrimage. 'The kingdom of God is within you.' Christ must reign supreme in the heart, and the SELF must die. Experimental knowledge had convinced her of the reality of it.

Among those who came to see her there arrived one day a Chevalier de Ramsay, reputed to be of Scottish stock, but a Chevalier for all that. Little enough is known about him, except that he had been in Cambrai, had met Fenelon the Archbishop, observed his manner of life, seen him giving away his considerable income with a free hand to those in need, opening his palace to refugees and wounded from both sides in the War of the Spanish Succession. He had seen a tall, thin, dignified figure moving with infinite compassion and humanity throughout his diocese, listening once a week with sympathy and deep understanding to those who came to make their confessions. The Archbishop of Cambrai had become a legendary figure in his own day, and through him the Chevalier had become a Christian. Now he went to see the lady whose influence on the Archbishop had been so great.

The Chevalier remained with Madame Guyon for quite a time, and during the course of their conversations the matter of her autobiography came up. Yes, it was still in her possession, though she had not added to it since she was taken to the prison in Vincennes. She had not really wanted to write her own story, had only done it out of obedience to her spiritual director, Father La Combe. It was the earlier part of that autobiography that had made so much trouble for her with the Bishop of Meaux, who had kept it for months before returning it to her. The latter part she had written because she felt it a duty to record the true facts of the case that involved others besides herself.

Would she be willing to have it published now, he asked? No, she would not. But after she was dead, it could be published. And so for the second time in her life she gave her autobiography into the hands of a man she scarcely knew, again with a proviso – not that its contents should be kept secret, but that they should not be revealed until after her death.

Before she handed it to him she read it through again, and as she did so felt a little uneasiness. What would be the reaction of those who read it against the persons who had treated her so badly? So she added a few more sentences at the end.

'I pray those who shall read this not to be angry against the persons who, through a zeal perhaps too bitter, have pushed things so far against a woman, and a woman so submissive.' They had been blind, had not known what they were doing. As she saw things now, the suffering they had inflicted had been necessary for her purification. And on that note she ended the story of her life. It was dated December 1709.

Chevalier de Ramsay kept his word, so he had the manuscript in his possession for ten years. She lived until 1717, two years longer than Fenelon. Her biography was eventually published in Cologne, in 1720.

Living Water

The fountain in its source
  No drought of summer fears;
The farther it pursues its course
  The nobler it appears.

But shallow cisterns yield
  A scanty, short supply;
The morning sees them amply filled,
  At evening they are dry.

Jeanne de la Mothe Guyon

Epilogue

A book, once distributed, is a lot heavier than thistledown, but it has a similar characteristic. One never knows where it will find its way, in what unlikely and remote place it will reveal its presence. It passes unnoticed over man-made boundaries, remains undetected for years, then takes root and flourishes. It may be discovered and stamped out in one place, allowed to blossom in another.

Several of Madame Guyon's books were published and distributed during her lifetime. Though they were eventually banned in France, nothing could prevent them being published elsewhere. Papal disapproval proved no deterrent to Protestant printers in Protestant countries. On the contrary, it provided welcome additional publicity. Her first little book on prayer, published almost casually in Grenoble, was being printed and distributed over the borders. The name of the woman the Roman Catholics would not own and the Protestants could not claim was known in many circles, and once her own story, written by herself, was released, there was no difficulty in getting it published. The slender thread on which it had been preserved through the years of her imprisonments and internal exile had held, and once it was released there was no stopping it.

There was no stopping the translators, either. An abridged translation into English was published in Bristol in 1772. In 1776 John Wesley produced *An Extract of the Life of Madame Guyon*, for although he disapproved of some of what she wrote, he handsomely admitted, 'I believe Madame Guyon was in several mistakes, speculative and practical too. Yet I would no more dare to call her, than her friend Archbishop Fenelon "a distracted enthusiast". She was undoubtedly a woman of very uncommon understanding, and of excellent piety. Nor was she any more a "lunatic" than she was a heretic'. He warned against the dangers of introspective mysticism, but he could not justly accuse her of being so preoccupied with herself that she forgot to do good to her neighbour.

About the same time William Cowper was lent three volumes of her poems, and was so impressed that he set about translating them. Some of them have been appearing in hymnals ever since.

Her books crossed the Atlantic, and early in the nineteenth century a Congregational theologian in the U.S.A. named Thomas Cogswell Upham was introduced to them. Her emphasis on the inner life of holiness found a deep response in his own heart. He believed it was no new doctrine that she taught, but that which reached back through the Reformation, through the traditional Catholic views on piety, right to the apostolic age when Paul wrote, 'I live – yet not I, but Christ lives in me.'

Having immersed himself in her autobiography and other published works, he wrote the book that was to be reprinted time and time again, right into the second half of the twentieth century – *Life, Religious Opinions and Experience of Madame Guyon*.

The fact that Thomas Taylor Allen of the Bengal Civil Service did not approve of the way T. C. Upham had interpreted his subject was all to the good in the long run, since it spurred him to the action of translating for the English-speaking family the *Autobiography of Madame Guyon* from the French.

And so the story of the woman who learned by experience that the Spirit of Jesus Christ can reign supreme in the human heart has come down through the centuries, reiterating the unchanging demand of a holy God: 'Be ye holy, for I am holy.' As for the suffering involved in the accomplishment of it, she herself might have written the words that came from the pen of a Chinese Christian imprisoned for his faith three hundred years after she was imprisoned for hers. They came out written on a flimsy piece of toilet paper, sent as a message of encouragement to his family, using a poetic form to conserve space.

Suffering often brings joy;
Daniel was tried in the den of lions,
Since days of old there has been order in suffering and joy;
After you have emptied the cup of suffering,
Then comes the cup of blessing.
How can a son not receive chastening from his father?
A gardener's pruning has no ill intent;
Only to ensure that the tree bears good fruit.
Without fire, how can impurities be separated from gold?
Without striking the iron, how can it become a tool?
Without chiselling, how can jade become a work of art?
Without pressing, how can grapes become wine?